Christmas Wrapped up!

© Scripture Union 2003

First published 2003, reprinted 2003, 2004, 2006, 2010

ISBN 978 1 85999 795 6

Scripture Union, 207–209 Queensway, Bletchley, Milton Keynes, MK2 2EB, England.
Email: info@scriptureunion.org.uk
Website: www.scriptureunion.org.uk

Scripture Union Australia
Locked Bag 2, Central Coast Business Centre, NSW 2252
Website: www.scriptureunion.org.au

Scripture Union USA
P.O. Box 987, Valley Forge, PA 19482
www.scriptureunion.org

Scripture quotations are from the Contemporary English Version published by HarperCollins Publishers, copyright © 1991, 1992, 1995 American Bible Society.

British Library Cataloguing-in-Publication Data.
A catalogue record of this book is available from the British Library.

Printed in China by 1010 Printing International Ltd

Cover design: Paul Airy

Internal design: Alex Taylor

Editorial team: Karen Evans, Judith Merrell, Anne Phipps, Amber Ross

Artists: Pauline Adams, Lynn Breeze, Anna Carpenter, Sue Cony, Gill Elliott, Wendy Hobbs, Brady Turner

Scripture Union is an international Christian charity working with churches in more than 130 countries, providing resources to bring the good news about Jesus Christ to children, young people and families and to encourage them to develop spiritually through the Bible and prayer.

As well as our network of volunteers, staff and associates who run holidays, church-based events and school Christian groups, we produce a wide range of publications and support those who use our resources through training programmes.

With grateful thanks to all the writers and artists who contributed to SALT 3 to 4+, 5 to 7+, 8 to 10+, 11 to 13+ and SALT All Ages. Without their hard work and creativity this book could not have been produced. And with our thanks to Scripture Union field and schools workers who have been willing to share their expertise and bright ideas. Every effort has been made to attribute items correctly, but we apologise to any author whose work has not been credited. Please inform the publisher and we will endeavour to put matters right in any future editions of Christmas Wrapped Up.

Contents

Introduction

Party ideas

Instant angel, page 53

Stand-up cards, page 57

Fold-up card, page 59

Advent banner, page 45

Put Christ at the beginning of Christmas!

Events

Drama

Christmas craft

Stories

Services

Additional resources

Introduction

Sarah is a young mum in her late twenties. She doesn't go to church, but she can vividly remember being an angel in her Sunday school nativity play and she feels sure that there is more to Christmas than the frenzy of writing cards and wrapping presents, shopping 'til you drop and eating 'til you pop. What can her local church offer her and her family this Christmas? How about a family-friendly Christingle service, a service that's not too long and not too wordy, a service that includes a superb take-home reminder of Jesus, the light of the world? Check out page 65!

Seven-year-old Sam can still remember the wacky games, the sticky craft activities, the wet sponge quizzes and the hilarious sketches that he thoroughly enjoyed for a week at the J Team holiday club. Next summer is a long way off and he'd love to see the leaders, sing the songs and relive the fun all over again. What can his local church offer him this Christmas? How about a Christmas fun day, a chance for the parents to go Christmas shopping without their children while the children remember the serious fun that they had at holiday club? Check out page 16!

The Johnson family has just moved into the area, they have hardly met the neighbours and they don't feel very at home. They've been thinking about going to a church, but feel nervous about 'just walking through the door'. Supposing they get the wrong time, supposing the kids make a noise, supposing everyone stares or they sit in the wrong place. What can their local church offer them and their family this Christmas? How about an invitation to Christmas services, delivered to them on their doorstep by carol singers bearing mince pies? Check out page 7!

Colin has a stressful job and he always has to work overtime in the run up to Christmas, but he also needs an instant Sunday group

Christmas party and some new craft activities for his group to make and take home. Sally, the new curate, needs to plan an all-age nativity service and she also has to visit three local schools to take a Christmas assembly. Pam needs a play for her class assembly and if she could use the same play with her Sunday group then that would be a real bonus... And so the list goes on.

In *Christmas Wrapped Up* we have put together some fresh new ideas, along with one or two old favourites, to bring you a resource book that will help you bring the true meaning of Christmas to your church and to your local community. At this time of year many people venture into church, perhaps for the first time. *Christmas Wrapped Up* offers activities, services and suggestions to help newcomers feel comfortable and at home within the church family. We hope that the familiarity of the Christmas narrative, told in a creative way, might enable more people to meet Jesus, Son of God and Saviour, and to see beyond the baby in the manger. *Christmas Wrapped Up* aims to explain the true meaning of Christmas in everyday, jargon-free language to enable people to move on from tinsel, trimmings and sentimentality to a desire to know why God gave us the gift of his son on that first Christmas Day.

You might want to take and use one entire Christmas service from *Christmas Wrapped Up* or you might prefer to take a couple of games, a rhyme, a short talk and a take-home craft activity to create your own Christmas fun session for the children and young people in your church. However you decide to use *Christmas Wrapped Up* we hope that you will dip into the resources here, adapt them and make them your own, so that the people in your church and community will get to meet Jesus – after all, it is his birthday that we are celebrating!

Judith Merrell

Quick ideas for Christmas evangelism

A few simple ideas to share the true spirit of Christmas with your community

Gift-wrapping service

If your church is close to a busy shopping centre, ask if you can set up a gift-wrapping table with sticky tape, scissors, gift wrap and ribbon. Offer a free, while-you-wait present-wrapping service to anyone passing by with Christmas gifts they've just bought. Take the opportunity to chat to people while you wrap a present for them. Send them away with an invitation to your Christmas services.

Carol singing with a difference

Get together a good-sized group of singers, preferably including some who can sing harmony. Go carol singing in the neighbourhood around your church, at your local shopping centre or in the supermarket (get permission first!), or, if your church is on a busy-ish road, outside the church on a Saturday morning.

Keep the singing fairly lively! In advance, put together a sheet of carols with some verses cut, so that you sing several different ones instead of just one carol at each stop.

Instead of asking for money, give each home a Christmas card from the church plus an invitation to your Christmas services. And why not offer a small gift such as a mince pie, a candle or copy of a Gospel?

Special services

If your church is in a busy shopping area, or by a local park, have a carol service at a time when most people will be in the area, eg Saturday afternoon. Advertise it well in advance so that people can plan to be there, and have people out on the streets the previous week and just before your service to invite the shoppers or those playing football in the park. Sing well known carols and cut out one or two verses so that they don't drag on. Aim to make any 'talk' simple and short (two minutes maximum).

Why not try a 'Happy birthday Jesus' party or a Christingle service (see page 65) for something a bit different that might appeal to those who don't worship with you regularly?

Video club

Hold an afternoon video club for children on one or two Saturdays in early December to give parents the opportunity to go Christmas shopping without their offspring. Make sure that you choose a film with the appropriate certificate for the age group. Stop the film half way through for a popcorn break and the chance to bend and stretch.

Holiday club reunion

December is a great time for a holiday club reunion! For those children who do not come to your church, it can be a very long time from one holiday club to the next. You might like to use one of the programmes suggested in our 'Christmas fun day' feature on page 16. Take the opportunity to remind the parents of all the children's activities available at your church and to invite them to any family-friendly Christmas activities that your church has planned.

Give away mince pies

Set up a stand in a busy shopping centre and give away mince pies to passers-by. Have sweets or chocolate Christmas tree decorations for children. Offer the adults an invitation to your Christmas services.

Face painting

Set up a stall in your local shopping centre with face paints, a big mirror, wet wipes etc. Offer to paint children's faces for free. Have two or three face designs on show for the children to choose from. Include one or two simple designs that don't take too long, eg a star stencilled on to the forehead, arm or cheek. While the adults watch and wait, take the opportunity to invite them to any suitable Christmas events at your church.

Link the chain

You will need: *strips of coloured paper; staplers; pens or pencils; a large strip of paper with the word 'JESUS' written on in big, bold letters*

Talk about all the exciting things that happen at Christmas. Ask everyone what they enjoying seeing and doing, eg singing carols, watching Christmas films on television, making mince pies, choosing presents, unwrapping presents, going to Christmas services at church. Give everyone a strip of coloured paper and ask them to write or draw their idea on it.

Divide the people into two groups and give them staplers to make the strips of paper into paper chains.

Finally, talk about what really makes Christmas important. What joins everything together? Produce the strip of paper with the word 'JESUS' written on. Use this to join the two paper chains together. Jesus is now in the centre of the chain and linking everything together. It is important to make sure that Jesus is right at the centre of our celebrations.

Marjory Francis

The example of the wise men

Talks can often be built around a simple concept. This and 'Seeking Jesus' are examples of this idea.

The wise men sought Jesus – we can seek Jesus too.

The wise men knelt down and worshipped Jesus – we can worship him too.

The wise men gave gifts to Jesus – what can we offer to Jesus? We can give him our time, our love, our money, our lives.

Let's follow the example of the wise men.

Seeking Jesus

The shepherds sought the shepherd.

The wise men sought the wise man.

And the star led them to the superstar.

Jesus is the good shepherd who guides us in the right paths, he is the wise counsellor and teacher, he is the real star at Christmas.

Colin Draper

Pillow talk

You will need: *a pillow and a sheet*

Tell the story of Christmas using the pillow and sheet as props.

Begin by using the sheet as Mary's dress as you tell everyone how an angel came to Mary and told her that she was going to have a baby.

Use the sheet and pillow to represent Joseph's bed as he goes to sleep after hearing this worrying news.

Wear the sheet as a cloak to represent the angel speaking to Joseph.

Return the sheet and pillow to Joseph's bed as he wakes up and realises what he must do.

Use the sheet as a train on Mary's wedding dress.

Use the sheet as Mary's dress and the pillow as padding to suggest her pregnancy, as you tell everyone how Joseph and Mary travelled to Bethlehem to register when she was heavily pregnant.

Wrap the pillow in the sheet to represent the baby Jesus as you explain how he was born in a stable.

Paul Wallis

Christmas belongs to Christ

You will need: *a big bag or box with Christmas items inside*

Take out items one at a time and ask if there's anything about them that might make you think of Jesus. For example: Christmas cards can carry a message of good news, and Jesus coming is 'Good News'; a Christmas tree can remind us that Jesus died on a cross; it is an evergreen tree and Jesus coming means we can be with God forever. Christmas lights remind us that Jesus is the light of the world; Santa Claus was originally a saint who loved Jesus. Some of these are pretty tough so be prepared to prompt!

Everything can lead us back to Jesus. The commercial side of Christmas without Christ is hollow. Now it is time for the church to reclaim the secular festival and show how every little thing can always lead us back to Christ.

Michael Eden

Light of the world

You will need: *one very large candle and seven smaller candles*

Invite six people to come to the front, making sure you choose a range of ages from the very young to the very old. Stand them in a line (in no particular order), give each person a candle and hold one yourself. Have a very large candle, already lit, at the front too.

Describe a town centre lit up by Christmas lights, or a house with twinkling lights, and explain that lights in a world of darkness remind us of Jesus, the light of the world. The big candle represents Jesus alive in the world today.

Light your own candle from the big one, showing that the bigger candle loses nothing in lighting another candle, but now your candle (and your life) has been set alight by Jesus.

Use your candle to light the candle of one of your helpers at the end of the line. Because you haven't kept the light to yourself, another candle has been lit and another life brightened up. But your candle has lost nothing in lighting another candle.

Continue until all the candles are lit. Explain that younger people can learn from those who are older and those who are more mature can still be inspired by the children. If any of the candles go out there will be less light in the room. If a candle goes out it can be relit from any of the others, including the one representing Jesus, the light of the world. We can all help each other, and together we can make a difference in the world.

Michael Eden

The meaning of Christmas

You will need: *9 large envelopes or paper bags each labelled with one letter of the word CHRISTMAS. Items associated with Christmas that begin with each letter of the word and that will fit in the envelopes, see below. Washing line and pegs (optional)*

Show the group your set of envelopes and ask them to help you make a word using the letters. You might like to ask two volunteers to hold up a length of washing line so that you can peg out the envelopes for everyone to see.

Explain that these envelopes are going to help you to discover the true meaning of Christmas. Pull an item out of each one in turn and talk about how it is relevant to Christmas. After each item say 'But surely there must be more to Christmas than this?' before moving on to the next one.

C – A Christmas card.
H – A piece of holly.
R – A picture of reindeer.
I – A list where everything begins with the words 'I want...' eg: I want a Lego racer.
S – A picture or decoration showing Santa Claus.
T – A picture or recipe for turkey.
M – A mince pie.
A – An Advent calendar.
S – Son of God, Saviour. A picture of Jesus in a manger or a model from a nativity scene. On Christmas day God's own son, Jesus, was born. He came to tell the whole world just how much God loved each and every one of us. Christmas is the birthday of the son of God, the birthday of the saviour of the world – he is the true meaning of Christmas.

Judith Merrell

Christmas wrapped up

A well wrapped party by Evelyn Stewart

The aim of this party is to give children a really enjoyable experience, while at the same time helping them to think a bit more about giving gifts, and discovering that the most important gift they can ever receive is God's Christmas gift to the world – Jesus.

Birthday gifts

Children are used to taking a gift with them to a birthday party. Why not describe this Christmas party as Jesus' birthday party and encourage the children to bring a gift? These gifts can be passed on to elderly people in the local community, or, if they are toys, passed on to a charity that distributes toys to children in need.

Depending on the circumstances of the children in your group, give guidance about the value of the gift. For example, you could set a limit on how much the gift should cost, or you could specify that the gift should not be bought – it could be either home-made or second-hand.

Invitations

Make sure every child in your group receives an invitation (see page 15) several weeks in advance to reduce the likelihood of children missing out because their family have made other plans.

Roll up each invitation inside a piece of thin card, then wrap it in Christmas wrapping paper to make a 'cracker'. Attach a gift label saying 'A Christmas invitation for _____'.

Prizes

Some of the games will have one or more winners. Keep the prizes very small and inexpensive, eg pencils, rubbers, sweets (see note under 'food').

Party food

If you intend to provide food, drinks or sweets, ask parents in advance for a written note of any allergies, or items that they do not want their child to be given. Keep food simple without too much choice and provide tables and chairs to sit at.

Starting off

It's always a good idea to have an activity for children to do as soon as they arrive at a party. This will keep the early ones busy until everyone has arrived and you're ready to play the first game. You could use one or both of the following craft activities.

Wrapping-paper hats

Give every child a piece of Christmas wrapping paper and show them how to fold it up to make a party hat. Have sticky tape, sticky shapes and scraps of tinsel available for decoration.

Christmas boxes

You will need: *copies of the box template on page 55; scissors; PVA glue; crayons*

Show the children a finished box, then help them to follow the instructions to colour, cut out and make up their own box.

Ideas for using the box:
☆ Put a few sweets in the box and give it as a gift to someone who is not at the party.
☆ Write 'I love you' on a piece of paper and put it inside the box. Give the box to a parent or someone else.
☆ Take the box away empty to use for wrapping a small Christmas gift.

 Younger children could be given a box that has already been cut out.

Pass the parcel on

Choose a small gift that can be shared by the whole group, eg sweets or stickers. Attach a note saying 'Share these with the whole group'. Add 10 or more layers of wrapping paper. On each layer, stick an instruction such as 'Give the parcel to the person with the longest hair', 'Give the parcel to the person with a birthday nearest to today', 'Give the parcel to the youngest person' etc.

To play the game, sit in a circle and pass the parcel around as music is playing. When the music stops, the child holding the parcel should take off a layer and follow the instruction. When the last layer is removed, the label should be read aloud and the prize shared.

Decorations dip

You will need: *a box and two each of six different Christmas decorations, eg tinsel, candle, bauble, star, Christmas card, angel*

Place one of each of the decorations inside the box and spread the others around the room. Play music and ask the children to move around or dance. When the music stops, the children

Parties

should choose a type of decoration and go and stand beside it. A leader, who can't see the children, should remove one decoration from the box. Everyone who is standing by that decoration is 'out'. Place the decoration back in the box and repeat. The last two or three children still 'in' are the winners.

Tip! Children who are 'out' for any length of time can get bored and silly. Think about how you can use this time constructively. You might want to have an ongoing colouring table where children can make one of the cards on pages 56–59. If the game is played just before tea, take children who are out off to wash their hands. Alternatively use the 'out for one go' method.

Keep your hat on

Use the hats the children have made, or give them each a party hat (without string!). Play some music and ask the children to dance. When their hat falls off, they are 'out'. To make it harder, call out instructions like 'move backwards', 'hop on one leg', 'touch your toes' etc.

Take a break

If your party is planned for at least two hours, then a restful activity in the middle is a good idea. You could watch a short Christmas video such as 'The Grumpy Shepherd' or 'Papa Panov'. Both last 12 minutes and are on the same video published by Scripture Union, ISBN 1 85999 017 7.

Tip! You could use this time to clear away a game and set up the tea table.

Musical Christmas cards

For this game you need a supply of old Christmas cards. It's always a good idea to keep a supply from one year to the next. If you don't have any, ask other leaders or parents if they kept last year's cards!

You will need one card for every child present. Scatter the cards around the floor and play some music. The children should dance around the room without stepping on the cards. When the music stops they must find a card to step on. In the first round, everyone should be able to find a card to stand on. When the music plays again remove one or more cards. (As a rough idea, remove one card for every ten children present.) When the music stops,

whoever has not found a card to stand on is 'out'. Repeat until only one or two children are left.

Wrapping paper jigsaw

This game works best with larger groups, eg 24 or more children. You will need one sheet of wrapping paper per six children. Each sheet should be a different pattern. In advance cut each sheet of paper into six irregular pieces. Spread the pieces around the floor and explain to the children that when you say 'Go!' they should go and pick up one piece, then try to find the other five people who have the same pattern of paper. They should then try to put their pieces together like a jigsaw. The winners are the group who complete their jigsaw first. If the total number of children is not divisible by six, some groups will not have a complete jigsaw. These groups should therefore look on the floor for their extra piece(s).

Christmas gifts

Buy some small Christmas tree decorations, the kind that look like tiny parcels. Buy enough of these for every child to have at least two. Make little gift tags and attach them to the parcels. Place all the gifts inside a shoebox and wrap the box. Place the shoebox inside a slightly larger box and wrap that. Then place that box inside a slightly larger box and wrap it. Repeat so that there are anywhere between four and eight layers of boxes. On the outside make a large gift tag saying 'The best gift ever'.

Show this to the children near the beginning of the party and ask if anyone has any ideas what the best gift ever might be. Invite a few children to unwrap and open the first box. Throughout the party, between games, open another box. Leave the last box until the end of the party. Give everyone a parcel (explain that it is a tree decoration before they try to open it!) and look at the gift tag. Explain that the best gift ever was God's gift to the world when he sent Jesus. Jesus wants to be our friend, he is always with us and always loves us. Other presents are good, but they don't last – Jesus will never let us down.

Christmas all-stars party

A very starry party by Fiona Walton

Star struck

Give out star-shaped invitations (see page 15) copied on brightly coloured card. Write 'You are a star!' on one side and decorate with sticky stars. Fill in the details of your party on the other side.

Shine like stars

Encourage the guests and leaders to wear glittery clothes, tinsel and decorations. But point out that there will be some running-about games!

Starshine

Go crazy with star decorations! They are available in abundance at this time of year. Hang star shapes from the ceiling, windows and walls. Use starry balloons and tablecloths and stick stars to paper cups. Sprinkle glitter or star-shaped confetti on the tables and provide a Christmas tree decorated with stars.

> **Tip!** When the children arrive there should be plenty for them to do. Set up game and craft tables for all to visit.

Star-t here!

Star printing

Have ready some star-shaped sponges or half-potatoes with a star cut into the top, silver, gold or yellow paint and plenty of plain paper. Help the children to print wrapping paper to take home. Make sure they put on an apron before they start and wash their hands afterwards.

Superstars!

Display numbered pictures of superstars around the room. Stick a strip of black paper across the eyes of each famous person to make the game more challenging. Use a selection of famous faces known by older and younger children (from David Beckham to Bob the Builder). Pair up older children with younger ones and provide each pair with a numbered piece of paper and a pencil. Ask them to walk round the room and jot down the names of all the superstars.

Face painting

Have a face-painting table where an adult paints stars, using a stencil, on to the faces of younger children and arm 'tattoos' on to the older children.

Party hats and Christmas tree decorations

Provide a selection of craft materials, eg tinsel, glitter, strips of card, glue, sticky tape, scissors, sparkly pens, star stencils. Invite the children to create a starry party hat.

Make star decorations for the Christmas tree using copper wire, ribbon, star stencils, silver card, glitter, sparkly pipe cleaners, lollipop sticks and paint. Provide a few examples of what can be made.

Star biscuits

Give each child a paper plate with their name on and a plain biscuit (Rich Tea biscuits work well). Help them to spread a little icing over the top of the biscuit and then to make a star-shaped decoration on top of the icing using chocolate buttons, Magic Stars, jellies and other small sweets. Put the biscuits on one side so that the icing can set and then give them to the children to eat at teatime.

Shooting (around) stars

Design an alien

Put the children into groups of three to five, and mix up the ages so that the older ones can help the younger ones. Give each group a newspaper, some sparkly pipe cleaners, tinsel, sticky stars, a cardboard box, a length of foil and some sticky tape. Challenge them to dress one of the group as an alien in just 10 minutes. Vote for the best alien.

Relay munch race

Divide the children into four teams of mixed ages, and stand them at one end of the room. Suspend four strings of five Hula Hoops from a long rope stretched across the width of the other end of the room, so that there is one string of food in front of each team. (Honey Nut Loops or Cheerios breakfast cereals also work well.) Make sure that younger children can reach the string of food. You will need one string of food for each child involved, but initially, hang just one string up per team. The first competitors run to the end and eat the food from the strings with their hands behind their backs. When they have finished they run back to the next member of their team while an adult replaces the string of food. The first team to eat their way through all their strings wins!

Be aware of any children with nut allergies.

Star hunt

Cut out lots of paper stars and put a score of 2, 5 or 10 on the back of each one. The majority of the stars will have the number 2 on the back, while those that are hidden more carefully might have a number 5 or 10. Divide the children into pairs. They must stay together for the whole game. One child holds a bag to put the stars in, while the other picks up the stars. At the end of the game count up the stars, add up the scores and award a small prize to the winners.

Balloon bash

Fill a bin liner with four or more balloons. Divide the children into two teams and sit them down facing each other with a small gap down the centre. Insist that the children stay seated for the whole game. The children have to use their hands to hit the balloon bag over the heads of the opposing team so that it lands in the opposition territory to score a goal.

Balloon bursting

Provide a chair for each team and a blown up balloon (you may need a few spares!) for each player. Put one balloon on a chair at the end of the room and divide the children into mixed age teams. Each player runs from the starting line to the chair, sits on the balloon and tries to burst it. A leader replaces the balloon whilst the player races back to the start line and the next player sets off.

Some small children hate loud bangs!

Star wars!

Imagine that your room is a spaceship. Label the four walls of the room Lazer zone, Flight deck, Shuttle bay and Sleeping quarters. Write these names on cards. When areas are called out, children must run there. Have further cards with commands written on them. When a command is called out the participants must take the appropriate action.

Asteroids ahead! *(Duck down and cover head.)*

Aliens approaching! *(Run to Lazer zone.)*
Warp Factor 6 *(Stand still and shake because you are travelling so fast.)*
Man the Escape Pods *(Run to Shuttle bay and grab a partner.)*
UFOs! *(Throw hands in the air and shout 'Don't panic!')*

An adult has all the cards, which he shuffles and calls out. Have a couple of trial runs, then announce that the last to arrive in an area or carry out a command will be 'out'. In a large group three children might need to be 'out' at once. To prevent those children who are 'out' getting bored, call out 'Return to spaceship' every so often as a cue for everyone to rejoin the game. The point of this game is to let off steam rather than to find a winner.

Star prizes

Have a bag of starry prizes. There are plenty of sweets with starry names: Galaxy, Starburst, Magic Stars, Milky Way, Flying Saucers. You could also use luminous stars or starry or sparkly hair bobbles or slides.

Star grazing

Provide star-shaped food. Use star cutters to make biscuits or to cut cucumber, ham, salami and bread to make star-shaped sandwiches. Put star-shaped cards on cocktail sticks announcing sandwich fillings. Make a star-shaped cake as a centrepiece and decorate it with indoor sparklers. Use star stencils to sprinkle icing sugar onto the top of chocolate buns. Make fruit kebabs and try to include starfruit. Stick the kebabs into half a grapefruit covered in foil. You might even be able to find an ice cube tray with star-shaped holes!

You can often hire star-shaped tins quite cheaply.

Follow that star

You may like to include a thought for the evening. Perhaps briefly tell the story of the wise men following the star to Jesus. Why not use the finger puppets on page 46 or use the background and figures from pages 47 to 49. There is also an excellent wise man rap on page 92. You could finish by singing 'Shine, Jesus, shine'!

A further selection of games with a Christmas theme can be found on page 84.

13

Stars galore!

Star printing

Aim: to experiment with star shapes
Activity: art activity
All you need: blue or black paper; silver, gold (or yellow) readymixed paint on plastic saucers/lids; a variety of star shapes in different sizes (eg plastic cutters, card stencils, potato blocks, foam templates), brushes; cover-up and clean-up facilities

1 Give the children the opportunity to experiment with creating their own pictures. Display in worship time at the end of the session.

Pipecleaner stars

Aim: a reminder of the Christmas story
Activity: craft
All you need: tinsel pipecleaners in a variety of colours (each star needs three)

1 Twist together three pipecleaners into a star shape. Add a thin cotton loop or simply bend the end of one pipecleaner over to make a loop to hang them up.

Star candleholder

All you need: clay or play dough, rolling pin; star cutter; gold or silver spray paint; adhesive and spreaders, glitter; small candle for each holder

1 Roll out the clay to 2 cm thickness.
2 Cut out star shapes.
3 Make a dent with the end of the candle in the middle of the shape to 1 cm depth.
4 Leave to dry and harden for a while.
5 Later stick on glitter or (adult) spray with paint. When dry, put the candle in place.

Shortbread stars

All you need: two measures of self-rasing flour: one measure margarine: one measure sugar; plus some beaten egg, lemon juice, yellow icing, sugar strands; a star cutter; adult to supervise cooking

1 Rub margarine into flour and sugar mixture; mix to stiff dough with egg and lemon juice. Knead well. Roll out thinly, cut into stars.
2 Bake on lightly greased trays for 15 mins in a medium oven.
3 Decorate when cool with icing and sugar strands.

Marzipan stars

All you need: packets of yellow or white marzipan; icing sugar, rolling pin; small star cutter; small polythene bags (kept well out of reach), cake decorations

1 For this, and any activity involving food, be alert to health, safety, hygiene and allergy issues.
2 Roll out the marzipan, dusting the surface and rolling pin with a little icing sugar to prevent sticking.
3 Cut out star shapes. Decorate with sugar strands, glacé fruit, small sweets, if you wish.
4 Allow to harden before putting them into bags for taking home.

Fondant stars

All you need: small tin of condensed milk, 1kg icing sugar; glacé lemon slices; lemon juice; yellow food colouring; star cutter; mixing bowl and spoon, small polythene bags; petit four cases

1 Work icing sugar into a thick paste with the condensed milk. Add a few drops of lemon juice and colouring.
2 Roll out and cut into shapes. Decorate with lemon pieces. Allow to dry before putting into paper cases; then put several into polythene bags for children to take home.

Christmas party invitations

All-
Stars
Party!

You are invited to shine at a Star Party!

You will travel to new worlds and meet strange new life forms!

Star date: _____

Planet : _____

Put the date in your starship's log now!

Dress in something starry or sparkly

 ## Christmas Wrapped Up!

_____

is invited to a birthday party to celebrate Jesus' birthday

Date _____

Time _____

Place _____

Please bring a birthday present!
For example, a craft, picture, biscuits, sweets or toiletries suitable to give to one of the elderly people in our community.

(Note to parents: please inform the leaders in writing of anything your child is not allowed to eat or drink)

Christmas fun days

Three fun day programmes by Helen Franklin

Planning

The best time for a Christmas fun day is probably one of the first two weekends in December. That way the children are not over-excited, nor are your team of helpers perhaps quite as busy as they may be later in the month.

Decide what is the maximum number of children that you can cope with, given how many helpers you have and what size room(s) you can use – and stick to that number!

Choose an outline, crafts, games etc (see Ideas section) and then allocate preparation jobs, purchasing etc. Arrange to decorate the rooms used to look festive and welcoming.

If you are putting the children into groups, choose names for the groups such as Stars, Crackers, Snowmen, Holly, Puddings, Trees. It is helpful for children to wear name badges; these could be made in the shape of their group name, or could be a simpler badge decorated with a picture of that item.

If you are going to invite adults to join you at the end of the time for refreshments and perhaps some carols, ask some of the church people who would not necessarily feel comfortable working with children, but who are good at talking to adults, to organise and serve the refreshments and be around to talk to parents.

Helpers

You will need: *people to do the following jobs (some can double up):*

Register children at the door
Maintain security at the door throughout the day (unless it is locked)
Welcome children and show them where to put coats, location of toilets etc before taking them to a group
Work with a group of children
Be 'up front' presenters/leaders
Explain and demonstrate craft
Explain and demonstrate games
Make drinks
Provide first aid
Provide music

Appoint an overall leader who would take charge in the event of an emergency!

Publicity

Christmas fun days are wonderful for children, but are also great for allowing parents time for 'those important pre-Christmas jobs that they want to do without having children in tow'! Make that a feature in your advertising!

Include a registration form as part of the publicity leaflet; this will save a lot of time on the day. You will need to know each child's name, address, date of birth, plus details of any allergies and relevant medical conditions, and who to contact in the event of an emergency.

Don't forget to mention that children will need to bring a packed lunch, if you plan to run over lunchtime. This is always easier than providing lunch because of the problem of food allergies.

In advance

If you ask children to pre-book for the event, put them into age-related groups before the day, so that it saves time on registration. Then keep an alphabetical list at the registration desk, and give each group a register of the names of their children.

All the timings given are only suggestions.

Programme 1
Christmas is coming!

Advertised as running from 10 am to 2 pm; doors open at 9.50 am to start registration.

You will need: badges; card for making Christmas cards; costumes and props for Mary, Joseph, shepherd and wise man; materials for your choices of crafts and games; TV and video; refreshments for adults and children

9.50 – 10.15 Children arrive, register and are given a name badge before being taken to their group to do an introductory activity, eg making Christmas cards (see pages 56–59).

10.15 – 10.40 All ages together.
Welcome
Song
Minimal rules (think of others, listen)
What's going to happen
Song

Mary's story – a simple re-telling of Luke 1:26–56 as if the storyteller is Mary. Script on the next page.

'When you've always lived in the same town, and you know everyone who lives there, it comes as a bit of a surprise when there's a knock at your door and you open it to find a stranger standing there. But that's what happened to me earlier this year! Perhaps that's why the man said 'Peace be with you', to stop me worrying. But it was what he said after that set my heart beating ever so fast! He told me that God was with me: well, that's always good to know. But then he said that I was going to have a baby! Well, I told him: I'm not even married yet! And he said that the baby won't just be my son, he'll be God's son, because the Holy Spirit would make him grow in me. Incredible, isn't it?!

'That's what my Joseph said – the man I was going to marry – when I told him. Incredible! At first, he wasn't sure that he believed me. The wedding was nearly off, until God showed him in a dream that it was all true, and that he should still marry me.

'Now we're off to Bethlehem, to register in the town where Joseph's ancestors come from. And the baby's due soon...'

10.40 – 11.15 If you have enough space and rooms, split the age groups for activities: infants do a craft activity while juniors play games.

11.15 – 11.30 Refreshment break, either together or served in groups. If you're staying together, you may want to show a short video during this time to keep the attention of children who are quick to finish. 'The Grumpy Shepherd' or 'Papa Panov' would be suitable – both are on the same video published by SU, ISBN 1 85999 017 7.

11.30 – 11.40 All together for song and Joseph's story, script below.

'So you know about Mary's news? It's amazing, isn't it? I couldn't believe it, and still find it hard to believe now that we'll be looking after God's son. He'll be born any day now and yet here we are, staying in a cowshed – not the best place for a baby to arrive, is it? Let me tell you why we ended up here. We arrived in Bethlehem where my ancestors came from, and I think all my relatives were here as well! The town was full and we couldn't find anywhere to stay. In the end, someone said that we could sleep in their cowshed – that was kind of them really, although it wouldn't have been my first choice for a bedroom! So, here we are. It's better than nothing. I just hope this baby's all right. What's that? (*Listens for a moment.*) Mary's calling me: she says the baby's on its way, that it will be born today! I must go!'

11.40 – 12.15 Infants play games; juniors do a craft activity.

Tip! Check out the Christmas theme games on page 84 and the selection of craft activities later in this book.

12.15 – 12.30 Together: quiz (see page 86) and shepherd's story, script below.

'It's a good life being a shepherd: looking after the sheep and lambs, helping them to find the best place to feed, seeing that nothing hurts them or worries them.

'It's a bit like that for babies too: they just lie there and sleep peacefully, trusting that their parents will look after them.

'Especially that baby I saw last night: he hasn't just got a mum and dad to watch over him, but God himself, and all his angels, because that baby is God's own son! And I've been to visit him! Let me tell you what happened.

'We shepherds were out in the fields keeping an eye on our sheep as usual when there was a bright light, and a loud voice talking to us. We were terrified – we couldn't work out what it was. But then the angel – because this was a messenger from God – told us that God's son had been born and that we were to go and see him. Us – just ordinary shepherds, being invited to be the first to visit God's son! And then lots of other angels appeared too!

'So when the angels had finished singing so beautifully we went into the town and we found the stable where the family were staying, and we saw him. Oh, he's a lovely little chap! A wonderful little lamb if ever there was one. We were so excited: we went off home singing and praising God at the tops of our voices. And why not – we reckon everyone needs to know about this special baby.'

12.30 – 12.40 Group game.

12.40 – 12.50 Wise man's story and song, see script below.

'Have you ever looked up into the night sky and watched the stars as they sparkle and shine so wonderfully? Do you know their names and their orbits, the shapes that they make as they move around the earth? If you do, then you will know, as me and my friends did at once, when a new star appears. And then the questions begin: where did it come from? Why is it there? What is its meaning?

17

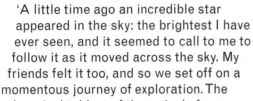

'A little time ago an incredible star appeared in the sky: the brightest I have ever seen, and it seemed to call to me to follow it as it moved across the sky. My friends felt it too, and so we set off on a momentous journey of exploration. The star's arrival told us of the arrival of a new king; we went to find him and to give him honour. But we didn't find him in a palace; in fact, the king there knew nothing about him and, we fear, will do something terrible now that he does know. We didn't find him in a grand house either. This baby had been born in a cattleshed and yet he was, we discovered, none other than the Son of God!

'We had brought gifts to honour a king and it was an honour to give them to this child and his parents: gold for royalty, incense for a Godly one and myrrh for – well, for death. But that will be a long way off, I hope, for this innocent child.

'God warned us, in a dream, not to go back to the old king. We didn't. And we hear that the family with the child have now left the country for safety. Yes, someone is looking after him all right: and that someone is God.'

12.50 – 1.15 Lunch. This will probably need to be eaten in family/friendship groups to allow for those children who have one picnic for all the family, not one each!

Towards the end, as children become restless, show a suitable video whilst others finish their lunch.

1.15 – 1.30 Christmas mega-quiz (see p 86), songs, prayer.

1.30 – 2.00 Parents come for refreshments. Afterwards, sing some carols.

 It's better to sing two verses of several popular carols than to sing all of one long one.

Talk briefly about the meaning of Christmas and invite them to other Christmas events and services. Wish everyone a happy Christmas and send them home with all their belongings, craft etc.

Programme 2
Ready, Steady, Christmas!

This outline involves each age group presenting a different part of the Christmas narrative. These should be planned in advance, but need not have scripts: they are ad-libbed or mimed, rehearsed though the day and presented at the end of the day to parents. Divide the children into age groups and allocate scenes according to the number of groups that you have.

For example, infant groups tell about Mary and Joseph going to Bethlehem and having to sleep in a cattleshed, about the angels telling the shepherds of the baby's birth, and about the shepherds going to Bethlehem to see him.

Junior groups tell about Gabriel's visit to Mary, about the wise men travelling to worship Jesus, and 'what it's all about', putting Jesus' birth in the context of his life, death and resurrection, and what God has done for us through this (script for this is at the end of the outline).

See 'Ready, Steady, Christmas!' on pages 38 and 39 for the full outline and script.

This programme runs for approximately five hours. The timings suggested begin at 12 noon and finish at 5 pm.

11.50 Registration and games that children can join in as they arrive.

12.10 All ages together.
Welcome
Minimal rules
What will happen
Song

12.20 Groups – talk through your scene and decide who does what.

1.00 Lunch

1.15 Video – choose an appropriate cartoon or Christmas story video to allow slower eaters to finish, and everyone to have a rest before running around again!

1.30 Songs

1.45 Juniors – games; infants – groups for craft activity.

2.30 Juniors – groups for craft activity; infants – games. The craft activity could be to make some 'scenery' or props for the group's part of the play, but ideally would (also) include making something to take home as a reminder of the day.

3.15 Groups – final rehearsals, finish craft etc. Parents come – 'Ready, Steady, Christmas!' is performed!

If you want parents to join in with songs, either provide words on paper or have them ready on an OHP.

Serve tea, orange squash, mince pies etc.

5.00 Home

Programme 3
Christmas Cracker!

This programme runs for approximately 2.25 hours.

On arrival (15 mins): Registration
Make a cracker name badge
Decorate a biscuit with icing and sweets

30 mins Games

30 mins Craft

10 mins Songs

20 mins Cracker hunt – do this in teams; write clues in such a way that each team can start in a different place and must complete the circuit of crackers in the right order.

About 1.75 hours after start: Parents return; serve drinks and biscuits.

Songs and cracker – pull a large cracker and talk about what it contains:

A surprise (the bang) – nobody expected God to come as a tiny baby, but he did.

A crown (the hat) – a reminder that Jesus came as a king, even though a baby.

Something to think about (the motto) – what God says to us through the Bible and through Jesus coming as a baby is something to think about.

A gift – Jesus is God's gift to us; what will you do with him?

World Wide Wonder – Jesus@Christmas

WWW – Jesus@Christmas

This presentation was originally an hour-and-a-half long Christmas event for Year 6 pupils, devised by Scripture Union schools' worker Wayne Dixon, and Jem Sewell of Slough Baptist Church. Over 5,000 pupils have already attended it at the time of going to press, and it's now running annually. It has been impossible to include all the details here, but if you would like more information on running an event like this in your church, or even to see a video of one of the presentations, please do contact either Wayne Dixon or Jem Sewell at Slough Baptist Church on (UK) 01753 523058, or email WayneD@scriptureunion.org.uk or Jem@slough.baptistch.net

Preparation

Write to schools you are asking to participate in September/October, to give them time to fit it into their schedule. Give details of how long the event will last and what will be happening. These invitations are more likely to succeed if they are built on already existing positive relationships and personal contact.

Be aware! The children you are coming into contact with will be from many ethnic groups and faith backgrounds. This must be taken into account when talking about Christmas, as some of the children may not be celebrating it. It may be worth taking advice from teachers on ways of handling this. Children will need to opt in to the session, and parents will have to sign a consent form.

You will need

• A booklet (already made-up) for each child (see info opposite)
• Enough home-made mince pies, uncooked, for each child to have one (check if the mince has been made with animal suet as this will be unsuitable for vegetarians)
• A few safe knives/utensils that the children can use to shape pastry
• A place to cook the mince pies!
• Lots of Christmas cards (preferably old ones!), with the fronts cut in half
• A CD player with lots of Christmassy CDs to play when there isn't a presentation going on up front. It really helps the atmosphere!

You need to make sure that your church is a secure place for the children to come to. Check the heating will be at a reasonable level, the toilets are safe and clean and everybody involved has been police checked. One person will need to be on the door as people arrive and will need to ensure that the door is secured.

Introduction ideas

Ask the children: what is the date today? How many days are there until Christmas? Ask the children if they are excited about the build-up to Christmas – mention presents and Advent calendars (how many doors left to open?). Find out from the children whose birthday is closest to Christmas (does anybody have a birthday in December? What date?) Bring the 'winner' to the front if he or she isn't too shy. Sing happy birthday to them and maybe give them a small present.

This leads nicely into talking about waiting for birthdays. How long does it take a baby to grow? Mary waited nine months for her baby to arrive, but the Jewish nation waited hundreds of years for a saviour to be born.

Hand out the booklets now and do the first page together.

Booklets

These booklets can have any number of quizzes, wordsearches or puzzles in them to give children something quick to do. The following items are essential parts of the booklets, as they'll be discussed from the front.

In the boxes below, link each item to the time span you think it takes to get it ready for Christmas:

Shops order Christmas cards – 48 weeks in advance

Farmers start fattening up turkeys – 15 weeks in advance

Shops put up their Christmas displays – 8 weeks in advance

Christmas number one single is released – 1 week in advance

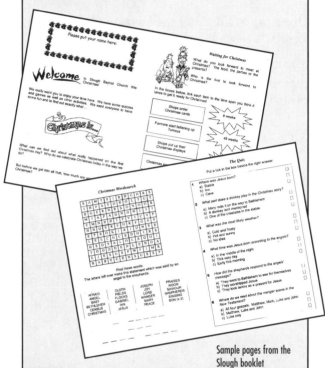

Sample pages from the Slough booklet

Quiz

1 Where was Jesus laid after he was born?
a) in a cot **b) in an animal feeding trough**
c) in a bed

2 What part does the donkey play in the Christmas story?
a) Mary rode it on the way to Bethlehem **b) A donkey wasn't mentioned** c) It was one of the creatures in the stable

3 What was the weather probably like?
a) Cold and frosty b) Hot and sunny **c) No idea!**

4 What time was Jesus born, according to the angels?
a) In the middle of the night **b) This very day** c) Early in the morning

5 How did the shepherds respond to the angels' message?
a) They went to Bethlehem to see for themselves b) They worshipped Jesus
c) They took a lamb as a present for Jesus

6 Where do we read about the manger scene in the New Testament?
a) All four Gospels: Matthew, Mark, Luke and John b) Matthew, Luke and John **c) Luke only**

Christmas survey

This can be used as a time-filler, and also to give you fun information about the children! You could make results charts from the answers given by the children who came, and send them out to the schools as a reminder of the morning.

1 What will be the Christmas number one? (Give some of the possibilities for this year – it's usually a battle between 3 or 4 favourites!)

2 What is your favourite Christmas carol? ('Silent Night', 'Away in a Manger', 'We Three Kings' or something else?)

3 What's your favourite ALL TIME Christmas hit?

4 What would you most like to RECEIVE this Christmas?

5 What might you be giving this Christmas?

6 What is your FAVOURITE part of Christmas? (Presents, parties, food, holidays, TV, being with your family, going to bed late, turkey, chocolate, something else)

7 What one hope or dream do you have for Christmas this year?

It would also be good to include in the booklet some fun Christmas facts, the answers to the questions (but in an unobtrusive place!), some contact details for your church and perhaps a little about the fact that the baby Jesus grew up – it's a good opportunity to mention Easter!

Time to make mince pies!

Tip! Remember nut allergies! You'll also need to check the ingredients are suitable for vegetarians. If your church doesn't have cooking facilities you could consider one of the crafts, or one of the 'cookerless cooking' treats on page 85.

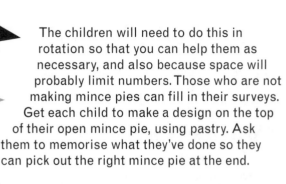

The children will need to do this in rotation so that you can help them as necessary, and also because space will probably limit numbers. Those who are not making mince pies can fill in their surveys. Get each child to make a design on the top of their open mince pie, using pastry. Ask them to memorise what they've done so they can pick out the right mince pie at the end.

Put the pies in a pre-heated oven and allow them to cook during the presentation. Have someone check on them once or twice and tell the children they're cooking nicely a few times, to remind them too.

Up-front time

Ask the children to imagine they're five or six years old, in their bedrooms and they're chewing bubblegum. They drop it behind the bed by accident and forget about it. Five years later (aged 10/11) they crawl under their bed and find a fluffy ball. They clean it off bit by bit... and realise it's their old bubblegum! They dust it off, put it in their mouths and start chewing. Eeew!

Relate this back to Christmas. There's lots of fluff added onto the 'bubblegum' of Christmas. Some of it is fine (presents, mince pies etc), but it hides what Christmas is really about. Tell the children you're going to try to work out what's the fluff and what's the real stuff of Christmas. Ask the children to answer the questions in the Christmas quiz booklet. Put those that finish early in groups, and give each group a pile of old Christmas cards, cut in half. They need to piece the cards together and then decide which are 'bubblegum' (an accurate Christmas scene) and which are 'fluff' (snow, robins etc).

Question time!

Introduce the 'man/woman who knows about Christmas', possibly in the guise of a nutty professor! This 'nutty professor' should answer the questions from the booklet. The children can ask them any question about Christmas and they'll answer it. If you're nervous about this, get the children to write questions on pieces of paper during the day and place them into a special questions box. Then you won't have to worry about thinking on your feet when difficult questions are thrown your way.

A retelling of the Christmas story should be an essential part of the presentation, perhaps using a series of visuals. The children could be asked to put some Christmas scenes from Christmas cards in the right order and then you could go through them telling the story. The

more interactive the better! See pages 8 and 9 for more Christmas talks ideas.

Finish by asking children to collect their mince pies. Check with teachers beforehand whether it's OK for children to eat them now, or if they'd prefer them to take the pies home.

Other ideas for the day

Get together some Christmas facts and figures to tell the children.

Use a rap to finish off the session (see pages 92–94).

The 'answers' to the paired-up Christmas cards (which are fluff and which are real) could be given up-front, maybe using Powerpoint.

Pass the Christmas parcels

An assembly talk by Claire Derry and Helen Franklin

Aim

To explain clearly the facts surrounding the birth of Jesus.

Bible base

Matthew 1,2; Luke 1,2 The birth of Jesus

You will need: *Christmas paper, a tape of suitable music and cassette player; a rubbish bag; the following items to wrap and number as shown:*

1 *A 'decree' – wording as suggested by Luke 2:1–3*
2 *A map showing Nazareth and Bethlehem (a simple drawing will do)*
3 *A 'No Room' sign*
4 *Some straw*
5 *A toy donkey*
6 *A doll wrapped up in cloths as Jesus would have been*
7 *An angel (a Christmas decoration or paper one)*
8 *A toy sheep*
9 *A star*
10 *A box to represent one of the gifts given to Jesus*
11 *A question mark*

Preparation

Wrap each item from the list in Christmas paper and number them in the correct order for the story.

Some can be omitted to cut down on time, but the larger number means that everyone should at least handle a parcel.

Introduction

Ask what games the children like playing at Christmas parties. Make sure 'Pass the Parcel' is mentioned.

Explain that today's game will be played slightly differently: all the parcels will be passed around together and, when the music stops, you will call out the numbers of the parcels that you want to be opened. Spread out the parcels among the children and give clear instructions about which way they are to be passed. When the music stops, call out two numbers at a time (otherwise it takes too long!) and have the children bring the parcels to the front to be opened.

As each parcel is opened, tell the relevant part of the story.

Story

(Begin with music. Open parcels 1 and 2.) Long ago, when Augustus was Emperor, he decided to take a count of everyone who lived in the country of Judea. *(Show the decree.)* Two people, Mary and Joseph, had to travel from Nazareth, where they lived, to Bethlehem, where Joseph's family came from many years before. *(Show the map.)*

(Music. Open parcels 3 and 4.) When they got to Bethlehem, the town was so busy with travellers like themselves that all the places to stay were full *(Show the sign.)*, and Mary and Joseph had to stay in a stable, and sleep in the straw. *(Show the straw.)*

(Music. Open parcels 5 and 6.) During the night, Mary's baby son was born. He was called Jesus. There was nowhere for him to sleep except the manger, the feeding trough that the cows and donkeys used. *(Show the donkey.)* Mary wrapped up Jesus in strips of cloth, and laid him in the straw. *(Show the baby.)*

(Music. Open parcels 7 and 8.) Jesus, the baby born in the stable, was not just any baby: he was the Son of God. Later that night angels *(Show the angel.)* went to tell the good news of Jesus' birth to some shepherds. *(Show the sheep.)*

(Music. Open parcels 9 and 10.) A special star came in the sky too *(Show the star.)*, and some wise men who studied the sky saw the star, and followed it many, many miles until it took them to the place where Jesus was. When they saw the baby Jesus they gave him special presents of gold, incense and myrrh. *(Show the gift.)* These gifts were not what you might take to a newborn baby; but they were just right for someone so special, like Jesus.

Application

(Music. Open parcel 11.) When the question mark is opened, ask the children why they think God sent Jesus to live on earth.

Explain that Jesus was God's special present to us, because he loves us so much.

Prayer

Finish with a simple 'thank you' prayer, perhaps with the children repeating, 'Thank you, God,' after each line.

From *Ready, Steady, Assembly*, published by Scripture Union, ISBN 1 85999 189 0.

Next, please

Suitable for: *smaller groups; older children or adults*

Characters: *King David, Isaiah, Micah, Matthew, voice (offstage)*

Scene: *The scene is a waiting room with three chairs for the characters to sit on.*

King David: Hello, is anyone there? I'm King David. I'm rather busy and I ought to be back at work, so if there's anybody who can deal with my request...
Voice: Sorry to keep you waiting. There's no one available to see you at present. Please can you wait?
David: I suppose it wouldn't hurt for a while. It's quite important. I've been given this wonderful promise by God, and I really must know when it's going to happen. I've been told that I'm going to be a famous leader and that one of my sons will be king after me. In fact, I'm always going to have descendants and my kingdom will last forever.
Voice: Sorry you're still waiting. You are currently third in the queue. Your length of wait should be about one thousand years.
David: One thousand years? A man could die of boredom...
(Enter Isaiah.)
Isaiah: Is anyone there? I'm Isaiah. The prophet Isaiah from Judah. I'd be grateful if I could see someone fairly quickly, as I'm very busy.
Voice: Sorry to keep you waiting. There's no one available to see you at present. Please can you wait?
Isaiah: It is important. *(Seeing David.)* You waiting too?
David: Yes, I've got to find out when God's going to keep his promise to my descendants. I've got a long wait by the sound of it.
Isaiah: I've been given a promise, too. I've been told a new king is going to come from among David's descendants.
David: *(Excited.)* That's me... that's me!
Isaiah: *(Surprised.)* What... the new king?
David: No, I'm King David.
Isaiah: Pleased to meet you. I'm Isaiah, and I'm one of God's prophets. He uses me to pass his important messages to his people. God told me that your descendant was going to be a wise ruler who would behave as God wanted. He won't make decisions on what things look like, or what others say, but will sort out problems fairly. It will be a time of great peace. Even the animals will get on with each other. Wolves and sheep and leopards and goats will all live happily side by side. And children will be able to look after them. In God's kingdom everyone will know and love the Lord. It sounds so exciting and wonderful that I need to know when this is going to happen.
Voice: Sorry you're still waiting. You are currently second in the queue. Your length of wait should be about seven hundred and fifty years.
Isaiah: Seven hundred and fifty years? A man could die of boredom...
(Enter Micah.)
Micah: Hello. Is anybody there? I'm Micah. The prophet Micah from Judah. I'm fairly busy, so if we could keep this brief...
Voice: Sorry to keep you waiting. There's no one available to see you at present. Please can you wait?
Micah: *(Seeing David and Isaiah.)* Are you waiting too? I've had an important message from God and I need to know when it's going to happen.
David and Isaiah: Us too.
Micah: God's told me that a special ruler whose family goes back to ancient times...
David: That's me.
Micah: ...will be born in Bethlehem. He's going to bring his people back together and rule them with God's strength and majesty. He'll care for his people like a shepherd cares for his sheep and everyone will live in safety and peace. I can't wait for it to happen.
Voice: Sorry you're still waiting. You are currently first in the queue. Your length of wait should be about seven hundred years.
Micah: Seven hundred years. A man could die of boredom...
(Enter Matthew with great excitement.)
Matthew: Hello, I'm Matthew. The writer of the first book in the New Testament. Are any of you waiting? Because if you are, it's happened. Jesus, descendant of David, has been born in Bethlehem. He's the king who is going to judge with justice and peace. Come and meet him.

Christmas shopping

A sketch by Andy Riordan

Suitable for: *larger groups; older children or adults*

Characters: *12 Christmas shoppers and an angel*

Scene: *A group of people with carrier bags, marching to the rhythm as they speak.*

All: We're Christmas shopping,

And we're not stopping.

Got to find the greatest gift for Christmas.

1: How about a video?

2: How about a stereo?

3: What about the latest computer game?

4: How about a fancy clock?

5: How about some Christmas socks?

6: All the things in here look just the same.

All: We're Christmas shopping,

And we're not stopping.

Got to find the greatest gift for Christmas.

7: I want some fancy food.

8: I want some Christmas pud.

9: I need a turkey that would feed an army.

10: I don't want Brussels sprouts!

11: I hope we're eating out.

12: I need a rest before I go quite barmy.

All: We're Christmas shopping,

And we're not stopping.

Got to find the greatest gift for Christmas.

(Angel stands in front of the crowd with a hand held out to stop them.)

Angel: Stop! *(They all halt.)*

I've got good news for you,

Tidings of great joy, it's true.

In Bethlehem a Saviour now is given.

Jesus Christ, God's only son,

Brings peace on earth for everyone,

And glory to God in highest heaven.

1: He says God's sent his only son,

2: A Christmas gift for everyone.

3: Let's go and find him now while there's still time.

(They all start marching again.)

All: We're Christmas shopping,

And we're not stopping.

Got to find the greatest gift for Christmas.

© Andy Riordan

To infinity and beyond

By Judith Merrell

Scene: *Chris, Holly and Ivy discuss the meaning of Advent over a cup of coffee.*

Chris: Right now we're in a really special season, do you know what it's called?

Holly: Yes, it's the season of Adverts, when all the TV channels start showing their advertisements for Christmas toys.

Chris: No it's not! We're in December which is the season of...

Ivy: The season of Advances, because today children up and down the land ask their parents for an advance on their pocket money so that they can buy some Christmas presents.

Holly: I remember now! We're in the season of Adventure because this is the time when Mary, already nine months pregnant, rode her donkey to Bethlehem and that was certainly some adventure!

Ivy: That doesn't sound quite right!

Holly: No, but it's on the tip of my tongue... ad... ad... adverb... ad... advice... ad... advantage!

Ivy: That's it! Today is the season of Advantage. Good food, lots of presents, a holiday from school, those are all pretty big advantages!

Chris: Just stop talking and listen... Today is the beginning of Advent!

Holly: ADVENT! Yeah, that rings a bell!

Ivy: Yeah! Jingle bells, jingle bells, jingle all the way!

Holly: Hey! I opened a door on my Advent calendar this morning.

Ivy: Yeah! But what does 'Advent' mean?

Holly: Little doors!

Ivy: Never! The season of Advent is the season of little doors? I don't think so!

Holly: Well my Advent calendar is covered in little doors.

Chris: Advent means 'arrival' or 'the coming'. It refers to the fact that someone special was coming on that first Christmas.

Ivy: We've got Nan and Grandad coming for Christmas, and Auntie Flo! They're special to me!

Chris: I'm talking about the first Christmas. On that first Christmas Jesus arrived, he was the special person that everyone had been waiting for. Advent is the time when we get ready for Christmas coming and think about the arrival of Jesus on that first Christmas day.

Holly: How long had everyone been waiting for Jesus?

Chris: Years and years and years.

Holly: But most babies arrive in nine months.

Chris: Ah but Jesus is special. God promised King David, hundreds of years before, that one of his descendants would always be king – and that king is Jesus. Jesus is the King of the whole world and his reign will last for ever.

Ivy: So did God tell David that he was going to be one of Jesus' great, great, et cetera, et cetera grandparents?

Chris: No, God simply promised David that one of his descendants would always be king.

Holly: David was probably only worried about his children and grandchildren being kings.

Chris: That's right! But God's plan stretched on into eternity.

Ivy: To infinity and beyond!

Chris: Exactly!

Drama

Operation good news

A sketch by Mary Hawes

Suitable for: *large or small group; older children or adults*

Scene: *Gabriel, dressed as an army general, is facing the audience in front of the other angels (as many or as few as you wish) who are dressed in combat fatigues or similar. (Makeshift wings strapped over the fatigues will add a touch of humour.) Gabriel will need a large map drawn either on lining paper or on an OHP acetate, and a stick with which to point.*

Gabriel: Right, angels, pay attention. Operation 'Good News' is scheduled for tonight. You've all seen the message which the Lord God wants proclaimed. You'll probably never take part in a more important mission, so I don't want anyone making mistakes. Angel Angela – what is the good news?

Angela: *(Stands to attention.)* That Christ the Lord is born, sir!

Gabriel: Very good. And who is Christ the Lord, Angel Alan?

Alan: *(Stands to attention.)* The only son of God, Sir!

Gabriel: Very good, very good. Now, your target for Operation 'Good News' is here – just outside Bethlehem. *(Points to map.)* It'll be night-time, so you'll need to keep a good look out. What you're looking for is a group of shepherds keeping watch over their flocks. *(Mutterings of disapproval amongst the angels.)*

Gabriel: *(Looks around at assembled angels.)* I'm sorry – there seems to be a bit of a problem. Angel Angela, what is it?

Angela: Well, sir, it's just that... *(Looks around at the others for encouragement.)*

Gabriel: Come on, angel, out with it.

Angela: Well, sir, this good news is about the Son of God, isn't it, sir?

Gabriel: Yes – and the problem is?

Angela: Well, the son of God is – like – special, isn't he, sir?

Gabriel: Yes – and?

Angela: Well, if it's special good news – why are we telling it to – *(Shocked.)* shepherds?!

(Other angels nod in agreement.) Why not to the important people – like the Pharisees – or the scribes – or even King Herod? I mean, shepherds aren't exactly important, are they, sir?

Gabriel: Think back to the message, Angel Angela. Who is the message of good news for?

All angels: All the people, sir.

Gabriel: All the people – and that includes shepherds. And the Lord God sees them as being just as important as anyone else. So they get the good news first, right?

All angels: Right, sir.

Gabriel: So – Operation 'Good News' is go. Best wings forward, best voices for proclaiming, and Angel Alan...

Alan: Yes, sir?

Gabriel: The words are 'Christ the Lord is born', not 'Whey, hey – it's Christmas!' Dismiss!

 Tip! In an outreach service adults who are not used to church may feel less sure about laughing in a service. You may need to reassure them that it's fine to laugh and applaud. Have some 'regulars' primed to set the tone.

27

Unwanted visitors

A rap sketch by Sheila Jacobs

Suitable for: *three fairly confident adult or older child actors*

Cast: *King Herod, Priest, Servant*

Scene: *King Herod is sitting on his throne, centre stage.*

Herod: I'm the king, I've got the power,

I snap my fingers every hour.

Got lackeys here and lackeys there,

I got those lackeys everywhere.

They bow and scrape

(Servant rushes on, bows a bit, and king waves them away looking disdainful; Servant goes to stand stage left. Priest comes on, stands next to Servant, and the two of them whisper together conspiratorially.)

And scrape and bow *(Points to Servant and Priest, who bow low.)*

They're scared of me, they are, and how! I'm the KING!

(Leans forward, scratching chin and looking worried.)

But lately I've had a bit of bother.

(Gets up from throne, begins pacing up and down.)

Someone told me 'bout these wise men

who've turned up in Jerusalem –

Servant: *(To Priest.)* Asking, 'Where is the child born to be king?

We saw his star and we've come to worship him!'

Herod: *(Taking his throne again.)*
These unwanted visitors are causing hassle here. They're causing lots of worry! They're causing lots of FEAR!

(Herod snaps his fingers, Priest rushes over to him.)

Herod: All right, Priest, what do you know? This Saviour King, a trick?

Priest: No, majesty, it's prophesied.

Herod: I thought so. I feel sick.

Priest: Years and years ago, ancient godly men told us that the Saviour would be born in Bethlehem. He'll be a shepherd, leader, and on that wondrous day...

Herod: All right, all right, I've had enough now, Priest. Please go away.

(Priest backs away bowing but stays on stage.)

It's pretty clear I've got to think up quite a sneaky plan.

I feel completely threatened. I'm not a happy man.

(Scratches chin, then brightens up.) Aha!

(Snaps fingers, Servant comes over.)

Go and find these Magi, bring them to my throne.

I want to have a word with them, talk to them, alone!

Servant: Yes, majesty! *(Exit.)*

Herod: I'll tell them, go and find this babe, and tell me when you do,

I'd really like to go and see – I want to worship too!

Priest: *(Aside.)* Herod's got a problem. Forgets he's just a man.

No one in the world can ever thwart God's plan!

If this baby's the Saviour, let us each and every one,

seek him for ourselves, as our visitors have done!

Drama

The gift

A sketch by Andy Riordan

Suitable for: *four adult actors*

Four actors in a line face the audience. The Narrator begins in the style of an interviewer; 1 is an ordinary bloke; 2 a well-to-do woman, 3 is 'Mr Cynical'.

Narrator: What does Christmas mean to you?

1: Eating and drinking all day.

2: Cooking and washing up all day.

3: Putting up with my family all day.

Narrator: Who are you giving gifts to this Christmas?

1: I'm just giving to my family and a few friends.

2: I'm giving a little something to all my relatives and neighbours.

3: I'm only giving to people who give me something.

Narrator: What's the best gift you're giving this Christmas?

1: I'm giving the kids a computer game.

2: I'm buying my husband a gold Rolex watch.

3: I'm giving whatever's cheapest in Woolworth's.

Narrator: What's God got to do with Christmas?

2: Nice people go to church at Christmas.

1: Santa Claus is really Saint Nicholas.

3: Saint Michael is the patron saint of returned goods.

Narrator: God came to be with us at Christmas. What can God give us at Christmas?

2: I'd like to see peace on earth.

3: I'd like five minutes peace.

1: I wish there could be peace.

Narrator: God gave Jesus, the Prince of Peace. Who is God's gift for?

1: For people who have been good.

3: For people who go to church.

2: For people who are Church of England.

Narrator: God's gift is for everyone.

(The three people step forward and come out of character.)

Narrator: For God...

1: The greatest being.

Narrator: ... loved the world...

2: The greatest number of people.

Narrator: ... so much that he gave his only Son.

3: The greatest gift.

All: Jesus is God's gift for everyone.

© Andy Riordan

Mission incredible

A sketch by Jenny Baker

Suitable for: *two fairly confident adult actors*

Characters: *The angel Gabriel; Simon, trainee angel*

Scene: *Gabriel is sitting having a cup of coffee in a heavenly café, reading* The Eternal Times. *Simon comes over to join him.*

Simon: Gabriel – hi! Mind if I sit here?

Gabriel: Not at all, Simon. And how are you getting on with your angel training?

Simon: Not bad – I passed my grade two flying exams and have started 'swooping with speed' lessons. And I've just done my first 'watching over sleeping children' practical.

Gabriel: How did that go?

Simon: OK – there was a nasty moment where I tripped on a Playstation on the floor and banged my head on the bunk bed, but no one woke up, fortunately. *(There is a slight pause – Gabriel goes back to reading his paper.)*

Simon: I just wondered whether you had heard anything about the top secret mission that's about to happen.

Gabriel: I thought there must be some ulterior motive for you coming to sit here – do you mean the top secret mission where God does something to sort out that lot down there? The top secret mission that he has had in mind all along but has only dropped hints about?

Simon: Yes, that's the one – well, have you heard anything?

Gabriel: Yes, I have, actually. *(Goes back to reading his paper.)*

Simon: And?

Gabriel: I can't tell you if it's top secret, can I? *(Simon looks very disappointed.)* Oh, all right. Everyone will know soon anyway. *(Leans over and confides very excitedly.)* God is going to send Jesus, his son, to earth as a human being, and I've been chosen to go and tell them that it'll happen in about nine months' time.

Simon: Wow – that is amazing. You must be over the universe to be given that role! I'm really glad I came to see you – you see, I just wondered whether I could get involved

somehow – I know I'm not fully qualified, but obviously it would be really good experience to play a supporting role. Can I come with you?

Gabriel: Simon, I'm sorry, but that's out of the question.

Simon: But won't you need lots of help? I could be one of the heavenly host doing the background music – my voice isn't bad. Or I could play my trumpet in the fanfare – I can nearly play four notes now. Or I could be one of your bodyguards, keeping the crowds at bay, while you make the announcement. Or I could keep an eye on the press conference and make sure everyone asks questions in an orderly manner – please, Gabriel, please, please, pleeeeeeeeeeeease?

Gabriel: Simon, you don't understand. There will be no heavenly host, no background music, no fanfare, no crowds, no bodyguards, and definitely no press conference. It's just me, on my own.

Simon: What? Are you sure? This is the most fantastic and amazing event to have happened since... well, probably since the creation... and you say it's just going to be you? Doesn't God want to make a big splash and make sure everyone knows about it? Maybe you read your instructions wrong.

Gabriel: Everyone will know about it eventually, Simon. But it's going to start small. I'm going to talk to Mary, a teenager in Nazareth. She will tell her fiancé, Joseph, and her cousin Elizabeth, and maybe a few others. And that will be it for the time being. Other people will know when the time is right.

Simon: Oh, I just thought... I mean, if I was God, I think I'd want to make sure everyone knew about my plan to save the world.

Gabriel: Well, Simon, you should know by now that God does things differently and his ways are best. I need to go and get ready now. *(He stands up.)* But I have heard that a heavenly host will be required in nine months' time – I'll put in a good word for you.

Simon: Thanks Gabriel!

Drama

Mission incredible

A Christmas narration for young children to mime by Cath Soulsby

This sketch can be performed in church as part of a Christmas service, by children and adults together. It can be adapted to fit any size of group, within reason.

Characters: (adult) two adult narrators, one angel; (child) shepherds, sheep, an angel, some more angels, Mary and Joseph

Props: No props necessary but the children can be dressed up as required. The children will mime 'being cold', 'being hot', 'fighting the wolf', 'being frightened', etc.

Narrator 1: Over 2,000 years ago, in a country far away, lived (any number of) shepherds. They were looking after their sheep. (Shepherds stroke sheep.)

Narrator 2: Sometimes the sheep would try and run away... but the shepherds always brought them back. (Shepherds and sheep mime this.)

Narrator 1: Sometimes the big bad wolf would come and try to get the sheep, but the shepherds chased the wolf away. (Sheep mime being frightened, shepherds being brave.)

Narrator 2: Sometimes in the winter it got very cold and the sheep and the shepherds would huddle very close together round the fire. (Shepherds and sheep mime feeling cold.)

Narrator 1: Sometimes in the summer it was very, very hot and sunny and the shepherds would give the sheep lots of water to drink. (Shepherds mime doing this.)

Narrator 2: It was hard being a shepherd sometimes.

Narrator 1: But sometimes it was fun.

Narrator 2: And sometimes – well, one time – it was absolutely amazing. It was a dark, dark, night and the sheep and the shepherds were all asleep. (Shepherds and sheep lie down as if asleep.)

Narrator 1: SUDDENLY...

Narrator 2: There was a bright, bright, bright light in the sky – brighter than the sun, moon and the stars put together.

Narrator 1: The shepherds woke up and were very frightened. (Shepherds jump up and act scared.)

Narrator 2: The sheep woke up too, but they weren't frightened because they thought it was daytime and just started to eat the grass. (Sheep wake up and mime eating.)

Narrator 1: The shepherds looked up and saw a bright shining angel – a messenger from God. (Shepherds point at the angel in wonder.)

Angel: Don't be afraid – I've come to tell you something really exciting! Listen, today, down in the town, a very special baby has been born. A very, very, very special baby. It's Jesus – God's own special son who will grow up to show everybody that God loves them. He will be the Saviour of the world. Listen carefully so that you know where to find the baby. You will find him wrapped up in sheets of cloth and lying in an animal's feeding box. I'm telling you this so that you know it is true.

Narrator 1: Then there were angels all over the place, singing and praising God because it was such an exciting and important night.

Narrator 2: When the angels had gone back to heaven, the shepherds decided to go and find the baby Jesus – so they did. (Shepherds get into a huddle and discuss things, then come to an agreement, break away and set off for Bethlehem.)

But the sheep weren't all that bothered so they stayed where they were and went back to sleep again. (Sheep fall asleep.)

Narrator 1: And you know, the shepherds did find the baby Jesus, just like the angel had said.

Narrator 2: And when they met Mary and Joseph and the special baby in the stable, they were really happy that God had told them about Jesus before anyone else. On their way back to their sheep they told all the people that they met about what had happened. They told everyone about the bright light and the angels and the important message about the very special baby and they danced for joy all the way home.

(Shepherds leave excitedly through the church saying 'Jesus has been born' to everyone as they go.)

In the news

A Christmas sketch by Katherine Hull

Suitable for: *large, mixed-age groups with time for some preparation and rehearsal*

Characters: *(Speaking parts) Announcer, Vendor, Editor, Marcus, Newsreader, Innkeeper, 3 shepherds, Angel, Doorman, 3 wise men, Patricus; 5–10 non-speaking extras, for crowds, shepherds, palace guards etc.*

The Editor and Marcus could be performed by puppets hidden behind a low screen about a metre high, with words attached behind the screen to help the young puppeteers.

Songs create useful interludes for moving characters around. Use a mixture of carols for the congregation and songs or carols performed by the children.

Announcer: We all know that there were no televisions or newspapers around when Jesus was born, but just for a while suppose that there were... How do you think the amazing events of that first Christmas would have been reported?
Vendor: Mail! Mail! Get your Evening Mail! Shock Tax Tactics! Emperor orders census! *(In the news office.)*
Editor: Ah, Marcus! Is that you slinking in? What time do you call this?
Marcus: Sorry sir, got a bit of a hangover, sir, that party I covered for you at the palace, sir.
Editor: Hangover! I think you need some fresh air to clear your head! I want you to buzz off to Bethlehem for me.
Marcus: Bethlehem?
Editor: Bethlehem... Don't look so amazed! It's this census. I want you to cover it from the family interest angle... The son of an old friend of mine, called Joseph, and his fiancée, Mary, have got to travel from Nazareth to Bethlehem.
Marcus: But sir...
Editor: But nothing! They're an interesting couple, very religious... a good couple. Mary's expecting a baby. Heard on the grapevine that there's something different – special – about this pregnancy... some story about an angel appearing to Mary to tell her that God will give her this baby.
Marcus: That's ridiculous!
Editor: Well, who can tell? Joseph would have dropped out of the marriage, but something happened to stop him doing that.
Marcus: Don't tell me – an angel appeared to Joseph too!
Editor: How did you know? This time it was in a dream.
Marcus: You expect me to believe that?
Editor: Well, I'm told that Isaiah prophesied

something along these lines.
Marcus: But that was seven hundred years ago!
Editor: So it's about time the thing happened then, isn't it? Anyway I want you to go down to Bethlehem. See if you can find Joseph and Mary. Be on the look out for... Well, I don't know what – just keep your eyes and ears open. And take Timotheus – you never know – I've got this hunch...
Marcus: Timotheus – the cameraman? Wow, I've never been on TV before!
Editor: No – and you won't get on it at all if you don't get a move on!

Song or carol

Newsreader: *(News headline music.)* Good evening. Tonight, as the Roman Emperor's deadline for the census draws near, thousands of people are on the move, returning to their forefathers' homes. One place that has been badly affected by the crowds is Bethlehem. Our special census-affairs correspondent reports from there... Good evening, Marcus – how are things tonight in Bethlehem?

Marcus: Good evening from a very full Bethlehem, as you can see behind me. The innkeepers are *very* busy but, ah, here's one now. *(Innkeeper bustles in looking flustered.)*
Marcus: Can you tell me how full your inn is?
Innkeeper: Full? FULL? It's full to bursting – I've never known anything like it! Brilliant for trade – just think of the profits! *(Rubs his hands.)*
Marcus: Have you any rooms left? What about any people who haven't got here yet?
Innkeeper: There are no rooms left – I told you, we're full. The only place left – if you can call it that – is my stable. I suppose a few latecomers could go there, but it's a bit small and smelly.
Marcus: Hmmm. Glad I got here in time to get a room. Well, thank you for your help. *(Innkeeper leaves.)* That's the way things are in Bethlehem – very full, very noisy and nowhere to stay, unless you fancy a small, smelly stable. My next report will be from the hills above Bethlehem to see how all these people coming here has affected those who live out of town.
Newsreader: Thank you very much, Marcus. We'll be having more reports from around the region in our late evening bulletin.

Song or carol

Newsreader: *(News headline music.)* This is the nine o'clock news with reports from around Israel. *(Music.)* First, we hear from our man in Bethlehem – Marcus.
Marcus: Hello. I am actually up in the hills above Bethlehem, with some shepherds. How are you coping with all the travellers?
Shepherd 1: It's made the sheep a bit jumpy.

Drama

Marcus: That sounds almost like a joke! Jumper – jumpy!!

Shepherd 2: We're all feeling jumpy – like something's going to happen. *(Enter angel.)*

Shepherd 3: WHAT'S THAT?

Marcus: This is amazing – a man in shining white clothes has appeared, suddenly, beside the shepherds. It can't be... it must be... an ANGEL!!

Shepherds 1, 2 and 3: Shhhh!!

Angel: Don't worry. I've got great news for you – the Saviour has been born in Bethlehem. You'll find him wrapped up in baby clothes in a stable.

Marcus: *(To the camera.)* The Saviour – born in a stable? *(Angel disappears.)*

Marcus: What was that all about?

Shepherd 1: I don't know.

Shepherd 2: But we're going to find out.

Shepherd 3: Let's go down to Bethlehem. *(Shepherds leave.)*

Marcus: *(To camera.)* This is sensational. Nothing like this has been seen before.

Newsreader: So, what happens now?

Marcus: It seems there is a special baby in Bethlehem. I'd better follow the shepherds and find him. This is Marcus, from the hills above the little, very full and special town of Bethlehem, handing you back to the studio.

Newsreader: We'll keep you updated with this exciting news throughout the rest of the evening.

Song or carol

Newsreader: Marcus? What's the latest from Bethlehem?

Marcus: *(Quietly.)* I am standing outside a small, dark and smelly stable. It's full of shepherds looking at a newborn baby. His parents are calling him Jesus. I'll just talk to the shepherds. *(Approaches shepherds.)* Now you're here, how do you feel?

Shepherd 1: Excited and happy.

Shepherd 2: God wanted US to see this baby.

Shepherd 3: His name is Jesus.

Shepherds 1, 2 and 3: Jesus means Saviour.

Marcus: Mary, Jesus' mother, and Joseph plan to stay around for a while. That's all I can report to you from Bethlehem on this night when the Saviour was born, so back to the studio.

Newsreader: Thank you, Marcus. If there's not too much going on now in Bethlehem we could do with you here. Reports are coming in of a new star that has appeared.

Song or carol

Newsreader: *(News headline music.)* Tonight we have a special report from the palace. And the astronomer royal, Patricus, tells us more about that bright star that appeared in the sky... Marcus.

Marcus: Good evening from Herod's palace in Jerusalem. There was a lot of coming and going today when three very special men arrived. I have the palace doorman here.

Doorman: Evening.

Marcus: Can you tell me who these men were?

Doorman: They were professors of astronomy, studying the stars.

Marcus: What did they want?

Doorman: They asked where the king of the Jews was.

Marcus: What did you do then?

Doorman: Well, sir. I only knows of one king, so I took them to see Herod.

Marcus: Herod must have been pleased to have such distinguished visitors.

Doorman: I don't know as he was. He looked very odd.

Marcus: Here come the three professors. Good evening, sirs. How did your business go?

Wise Man 1: We are truly grateful. We have had so much help.

Wise Man 2: King Herod was most kind. He asked lots of questions about this star.

Wise Man 3: But there doesn't seem to have been a new king born around here recently.

Marcus: So what are you going to do? You've come all this way for nothing.

Wise Man 1: Oh no! King Herod asked his advisors and they looked in the old Jewish books. It says in Micah that there would be a king born in Bethlehem.

Marcus: Bethlehem!

Wise Man 2: Indeed. The star appears in that part of the sky, so we're going to Bethlehem.

Marcus: What will you do when you get to Bethlehem?

Wise Man 3: We shall see where the star stops and there we shall find the baby.

Wise Man 1: We have some presents for him. *(Wise Men exit.)*

Marcus: This is all very exciting. Patricus, what can you tell us about the star?

Patricus: The star appeared in the east, where the professors saw it. I have never seen anything like it before.

Marcus: Why did it appear?

Patricus: The professors are sure it shows the birth of a very, very special baby.

Marcus: They are going to Bethlehem. I was there a while back – during the census. I saw a baby in a stable. An angel had told some shepherds to go and see him. They were told that he is to be the Saviour. What does it all mean?

Patricus: It's simple really. God is fulfilling his promises in this baby. Babies grow up. I wonder what this baby will do when he's grown up!

(While Marcus and Patricus are having this conversation the children can come on stage for a final nativity tableau scene.)

Announcer: Jesus grew up to be God's perfect man – a pattern for us. He spoke about God's kingdom, healed people and went about doing good things.

Final song or carol

This is how it happened

A sketch by Kathleen Crawford

Suitable for: *large groups of children; does not require practise. This is an easy-to-adapt presentation which, in its basic form, requires little practise other than by the narrator and adult helpers. It can be as simple or as complicated as you like. You could dress up the main characters, use mime or speech, and move around the church as the story is told! It encourages everyone to listen carefully for key words in the story and therefore keeps their attention. It would be suitable for a church, pre-school or nursery presentation.*

A re-telling of the Christmas story from Luke 2:1–20 and Matthew 2:1–11

Characters: *Narrator(s), Stars, Angels (adults are required to lead the Stars and Angels)*

Other roles: *sound effects crew (2–3 people), someone to operate the overhead projector*

You'll also need: *(optional) nativity or crib scene displayed centrally at the front of church*

Props: *hammer, three wood blocks – one containing two large nails; coconut shell halves or two flowerpots; 1–3 sheep sound drums (the sort that you turn over and makes a 'Baaa' noise when you turn it up the right way again); a drum and drumsticks; several maracas; OHP acetates – photocopy (enlarge if necessary) colour illustrations of five or six suitable nativity scenes from Christmas cards or books, unless you are artistic enough to draw your own. Put on screen at the relevant points in the story*

Headbands for stars: *Cut an A2 sheet of silver metallic card into strips horizontally. Glue on confetti metal stars and a central silver star with a small piece of silver tinsel attached to the centre of it with double-sided tape. Staple or tape headbands to a suitable size for the children taking part.*

Headbands for angels: *Use gold card and cut strips as above for basic headbands. Fasten a 10–15cm strip of double-sided tape to the centre of the headband and attach a piece of gold tinsel to it. You should be able to make 11 headbands from an A2 sheet of metallic card. Alternatively, you could make some circles of gold or silver tinsel and just tape the ends.*

Stars: *Whenever the word 'star(s)' is mentioned, that group have to say 'Twinkle, twinkle' and open and close their fingers and thumbs.*

Angels: *Whenever the word 'angel(s)' is mentioned, that group move their arms sideways and outwards like wings and say 'Alleluia'.*

Sheep: *Whenever the word 'sheep' is mentioned the sound drum(s) should be turned upright in front of a microphone. (Instruct the sound effects crew beforehand and let them practise so that the timing is right.)*

Size of performing group: *The minimum is 5–6 adults/older children and an open invitation to all the younger children, including any visitors, who would like to join in. The emphasis should be on telling the story together rather than on having a small group of regular church members performing for the visitors.*

Narrator: *Christmas is a time when we remember how Jesus, God's son, was born in a stable in Bethlehem. This afternoon we are going to tell the story of Jesus' birth together.*

(Explain and demonstrate the part the angels and stars will play and ask for volunteers.)

So, this is how it happened...

A long time ago, a girl called Mary and a man named Joseph were travelling to a small town called Bethlehem. The Emperor's soldiers *(Marching drum beats.)* had told everyone that they must go back to the place where they were born so that they and their family could be counted. Joseph worked as a carpenter in Nazareth. He sawed wood and hammered nails *(Hammer nails into wood block.)* and made furniture for people to buy. It was a long, long way to travel from their home to Bethlehem and Mary rode on a donkey along the rough, bumpy roads. *(Bang coconut shells or flowerpots.)* Tiny stars were twinkling in the night sky when, at last, the lights of Bethlehem appeared in the distance. 'Nearly there,' said Joseph. Mary was very tired. She knew that it would not be long now before her baby was born. There were crowds of people everywhere, jostling and bustling in the streets. *(Shake maracas; sound of voices.)*

Joseph knocked on the door of an inn. *(Bang two wood blocks together.)*

'Have you any rooms, please?' he asked the innkeeper.

The man shook his head. 'Sorry,' he said, 'we're full up.'

Drama

Joseph knocked on another door. *(Bang two wood blocks together.)*

'Have you any rooms?' he asked the innkeeper. 'Sorry,' said the man, 'we're full.'

He tried another *(Wood blocks.)*, and another *(Wood blocks.)*, and another *(Wood blocks.)*. All the inns were full. There was nowhere for them to stay.

'What are we going to do?' asked Mary. 'The baby will be born soon.'

Joseph knocked on another door. *(Bang two wood blocks together.)*

'Have you any rooms?' he asked the innkeeper.

'No,' answered the man, 'but there is a stable at the back of my inn, where I keep my animals. It's warm and dry in there and you could rest on the hay, if you like.'

'Thank you,' said Mary and Joseph gratefully. 'That's very kind of you.'

That night, Mary's baby boy was born. She cuddled him gently and wrapped him snugly in pieces of cloth to keep him warm. Then she used the animals' wooden feeding trough as a cradle. Mary looked at her baby and smiled. He was so beautiful. She called him Jesus.

Outside the stable, the **stars** shone brightly in the night sky. It was a bitterly cold night. Not far away, some shepherds on a hillside were looking after their **sheep**. The men pulled their cloaks around themselves and tried to keep warm. Suddenly, a dazzling light appeared in the sky and an **angel** appeared. The shepherds were very frightened – they had never seen an **angel** before. All they usually saw were **sheep**.

'Don't be afraid,' the **angel** told them. 'I have come to tell you some wonderful news. Tonight a very special baby has been born in Bethlehem. He is God's son. You will find him in Bethlehem lying in a bed of hay.'

Then lots and lots of other **angels** appeared in the sky. They sang 'Praise to God in heaven! Peace on earth to everyone who pleases God.' The shepherds rubbed their eyes. They could not believe that this was happening to them. It all seemed like a dream. 'We must go to Bethlehem and see this baby,' they said. So the men made sure their **sheep** were safe and ran quickly down the hillside into the town.

Soon they found the stable where Mary and Joseph and the baby were. The shepherds stayed for a little while and then they went back up the hillside to look after their **sheep**.

The shepherds were so happy and excited that they sang and talked all the way home. 'God's son has been born tonight,' they said. 'It has happened just like the angels told us it would.'

A long way away from Bethlehem, some very clever men stood looking at the sky. They had noticed a new, very bright **star** and they were sure that it meant that something special had happened. They looked in their scrolls. 'It means a new king has been born,' they said. 'We must go and look for him.' So they chose some special presents, climbed on their camels and set off across the desert to find the baby king. *(Gently bang coconut shells or flowerpots.)* It was a very long journey.

The wise men thought kings always lived in palaces, but they couldn't find the baby in the big palace in Jerusalem. So they kept on following the big, bright **star** as it moved across the sky until, at last, it stopped above the house where Mary and Joseph and Jesus were. Then the wise men climbed off their camels and went inside.

They knew that the baby they were looking at was a very special baby. This baby was God's son. The wise men knelt down and gave him the presents they had brought – gold, frankincense and myrrh. They were very special presents for a very special baby.

When the wise men had left, Mary cuddled Jesus in her arms and smiled. She remembered the time when an **angel** had told her that she was going to have a baby and that the baby would be God's son. She thought about the shepherds and the message the **angels** had told them as they looked after their **sheep**. She thought about the wise men and the bright **star** they had seen in the sky. 'And now he's here,' she said to herself, 'and this is how it happened!'

This is how it happened

Countdown to Christmas

By Andy Riordan and Dave Shailer

Suitable for: *mixed-age groups*

Characters: *four Narrators, 10 chorus members.*

Scene: *Nativity tableau (optional): Mary, Joseph, shepherds, angel, Herod and his advisors, wise men.*

Two Narrators should be positioned on either side of the stage with microphones.

The chorus (10 children) should be positioned, upstage right and left, five on each side.

The characters in the nativity tableau should enter as indicated in the text and take up their positions centre stage.

Adjust the number of days and shopping days until Christmas to suit the date when you perform this sketch.

This sketch uses Bible readings from the Contemporary English Version.

Nar 1: Countdown to Christmas.
Chorus: *(Together.)* 10, 9, 8, 7, 6, 5, 4, 3, 2, 1, zero.
Nar 2: What do you count at Christmas?
Chorus 1: Ten cards I've got to send.
Chorus 2: Nine relatives coming to stay.
Chorus 3: Eight pounds of potatoes to peel.
Chorus 4: Seven days till Christmas day.
Chorus 5: Six presents still to buy.
Chorus 6: Five more shopping days to go.
Chorus 7: Four gifts I have to wrap.
Chorus 8: Three films I can video.
Chorus 9: Two fairy lights have blown.
Chorus 10: One more chance to see *The Sound of Music*.
Nar 1: What really counted the first Christmas?
Chorus 1: 10
Chorus 2: 9
Chorus 3: 8
Chorus 4: 7
Chorus 5: 6
Chorus 6: 5
Chorus 7: 4
Chorus 8: 3
Chorus 9: 2
Chorus 10: 1
Nar 3: It is the year AD 0. Well, approximately!
Nar 4: The Roman Emperor Augustus wanted to know how many people were in his empire.
Nar 1: So everyone had to be counted.
Chorus 1: 1
Chorus 2: 2
Chorus 3: 3
Chorus 4: 4
Chorus 5: 5
Nar 2: Everyone had to be counted, in Roman numerals!
(Chorus recite i, two i, three i, etc.)
Chorus 6: i
Chorus 7: ii
Chorus 8: iii
Chorus 9: iv
Chorus 10: v
Nar 3: Everyone had to go to their home town to be counted.
Nar 4: So Joseph had to leave Nazareth and go all the way to Bethlehem.
(Mary and Joseph enter from the rear and move towards the stage.)
Nar 1: Long ago Bethlehem had been King David's home town, and Joseph went there because he was from David's family.
Nar 2: Mary was engaged to Joseph and travelled with him to Bethlehem.
Nar 3: She was soon going to have a baby and while they were there she gave birth to her first born son.
(Mary and Joseph reach stage, place 'baby' in manger.)
Nar 4: She wrapped him in strips of cloth and laid him in a manger, because there was no room for them in the inn.

Sing 'Away in a manger'

(Enter shepherds stage left.)
Nar 1: That night in the fields near Bethlehem, some shepherds were trying to stay awake, counting their sheep.
Chorus 1: 1
Chorus 2: 2
Chorus 3: 3
Chorus 4: 4
Chorus 5: 5
Chorus 6: *(Increasingly sleepy.)* ...6
Chorus 7: *(Yawn.)* ...7
Chorus 8: Mmmm 8
Chorus 9: Nnnnnnnine
Chorus 10: *(Snores.)*
(Shepherds all doze off.)
Nar 2: All at once an angel came down to them from the Lord.
(Enter angel. Shepherds wake with a start.)
Nar 3: And the brightness of the Lord's glory flashed around them.
(Lighting effects.)
Nar 4: The shepherds were frightened.
(Shepherds tremble.) But the angel said:
Nar 1: 'Don't be afraid! I have good news for you, which will make everyone happy.'
Nar 2: 'This very day in King David's home

town a Saviour was born for you. He is Christ the Lord.'

Nar 3: 'You will know who he is, because you will find him dressed in baby clothes and lying on a bed of hay.'

Nar 4: Suddenly many other angels came down from heaven, and joined in praising God.

Chorus 6: 1,000

Chorus 7: 2,000

Chorus 8: 3,000

Chorus 9: 4,000

Chorus 10: Millions of angels!

Nar 1: They said:

Nar 2, 3 and 4: 'Praise God in heaven! Peace on earth to everyone who pleases God.'

Nar 3: After the angels had gone back to heaven the shepherds said to each other:

Nar 4: 'Let's go to Bethlehem and see what the Lord has told us about.'

(Shepherds move centre stage to join Mary and Joseph.)

Nar 1: They hurried off and found Mary and Joseph, and the baby lying in a manger.

Nar 2: When the shepherds saw Jesus they told his parents what the angels had said about him.

Nar 3: Everyone listened and were surprised.

Sing 'While shepherds watched'

(Enter Herod and advisors stage right.)

Nar 4: When Jesus was born in Bethlehem, Herod was king.

Nar 1: Some wise men from the east came to Jerusalem.

(Enter wise men.)

Chorus 1: One

Chorus 2: Two

Chorus 3: Three wise men.

Nar 1: No, just some wise men, it doesn't say how many.

Nar 2: The wise men asked Herod:

Nar 3: 'Where is the child born to be king of the Jews? We saw his star in the east and have come to worship him.'

Nar 4: When King Herod heard about this he was worried and so was everyone else in Jerusalem. He asked the chief priests:

Nar 1: 'Where will the Messiah be born?'

Nar 4: They told him:

Nar 2: 'He will be born in Bethlehem.'

Nar 4: Herod told the wise men:

Nar 1: 'Go to Bethlehem and search carefully for the child. As soon as you find him let me know.'

Nar 4: The wise men listened to what the king said and then left.

(Wise men move centre stage and join Mary and Joseph.)

Nar 1: The star they had seen went ahead of them, until it stopped over the place where the child was.

Nar 2: The men saw the child with Mary, his mother, and knelt down and worshipped him.

Nar 3: They took out their gifts: Gold,

Nar 4: Frankincense,

Nar 1: And myrrh.

(Tableau freezes.)

Chorus 1: 1999

Chorus 2: 2000

Chorus 3: 2001

Chorus 4: 2002

Chorus 5: 2003

Nar 1: About two thousand years have passed since that first Christmas.

Nar 2: Countless armies have marched to war.

Nar 3: Countless books have been written.

Nar 4: Countless politicians have made laws.

Nar 1: But none of them has affected the world as much as the birth of this one man.

Chorus: *(Together.)* 10, 9, 8, 7, 6, 5, 4, 3, 2, 1.

Nar 2: What do you count at Christmas?

Chorus 1: Ten cards I've got to send.

Chorus 2: Nine relatives coming to stay.

Chorus 3: Eight pounds of potatoes to peel.

Chorus 4: Seven days till Christmas day.

Chorus 5: Six presents still to buy.

Chorus 6: Five more shopping days to go.

Chorus 7: Four gifts I have to wrap.

Chorus 8: Three films I can video.

Chorus 9: Two fairy lights have blown.

Chorus 10: One more chance to see *The Sound of Music.*

Nar 1: What really counts this Christmas is knowing Jesus.

© Andy Riordan and Dave Shailer

Ready, steady Christmas

A Christmas play for children by Helen Franklin

This could be rehearsed and performed as part of the Ready, steady, Christmas! fun day (see pages 18 and 19). Alternatively use it as a class assembly or Sunday group nativity play. But how about trying it as an 'instant' nativity play? Do some minimal rehearsal before you start, and with hand gestures, indicate where various places are – Mary's home, the cattleshed, the fields, Herod's palace etc, but otherwise just give actors brief directions as they go along.

Ideas for music that might suit a range of ages are given, but choose what is best for your participants.

Scene 1: Gabriel tells Mary that she will have a baby; Joseph is told in a dream to marry her.

Song: 'Here we go up to Bethlehem' or 'The angel Gabriel from heaven came'.

Scene 2: Mary and Joseph go to Bethlehem and look for somewhere to stay. Jesus is born.

Song: 'Innkeeper, Innkeeper, have you any room?' or 'Once in Royal David's city' (vs 1,2).

Scene 3: Angels tell the shepherds about the baby.

Song: 'It was on a starry night' or 'While shepherds watched'.

Scene 4: The shepherds go to the stable to visit the baby.

Song: 'Mary had a little baby' or 'Angels from the realms of glory'.

Scene 5: Wise men come to worship Jesus.

Song: 'Come and join the celebration' (chorus, verse 2, chorus).

Scene 6: Why it happened and what it means.

The script

Scene 1

The annunciation to Mary, and Joseph's dream.

Speaking: *Narrator, Gabriel, Mary, Joseph*

Acting: *Gabriel, Mary, Joseph*

Narrator: In the town of Nazareth, lived a girl named Mary *(Enter Mary.)*, who was engaged to be married to Joseph, the local carpenter. One day, as Mary worked in her home *(Sweeps the floor.)*, a stranger came to the door. *(Gabriel enters.)*

Gabriel: Hello, Mary! God is with you!

Narrator: Mary didn't know the person, nor what these words meant, but she found out very soon! God's messenger was an angel called Gabriel, and he had some incredible news.

Gabriel: Don't be afraid, Mary – God is pleased with you. You will have a son. His name will be Jesus and he will be called 'Son of the Most High God'.

Mary: But I'm not even married!

Narrator: So Gabriel explained it all. The child would be God's son. Nothing is impossible for God!

Mary: I am the Lord's servant. Let it happen as you have said. *(Gabriel exits one way and Joseph enters the other.)*

Narrator: But when Joseph heard the news he decided to end their engagement quietly. *(Joseph shakes his head and turns away from Mary. She exits. Joseph sits down and falls asleep.)* But while he was still thinking about it, God sent an angel to talk to him in a dream. *(Gabriel enters.)*

Gabriel: Joseph, don't worry about it all – God is in control. The baby is his son. Get married to Mary and, when the baby is born, call him Jesus. It means 'Saviour' and he will save his people from the wrong things they do. *(Gabriel exits. Joseph wakes; Mary enters.)*

Narrator: So Joseph obeyed God and was married to Mary. And when the Emperor's decree demanded that everyone went to register in the town of their ancestors, Mary and Joseph set off for Bethlehem. *(Both leave.)*

Scene 2

Mary and Joseph go to Bethlehem and look for somewhere to stay.

Speaking: *Narrator, Joseph, Mary, Innkeeper, Chorus*

Acting: *Joseph, Mary, Innkeeper*

(Mary and Joseph enter.)

38

Joseph: Mary, we're here – this is Bethlehem!

Mary: Do you think we'll find somewhere to stay?

Joseph: I don't know – it looks very busy. I'm from a big family and they'll all be here. Let's try here. (*He mimes knocking on a door at various places, as the Chorus say the rhyme.*)

Chorus 1: Knock, knock!

Chorus 2: Who's there?

Chorus 1: Mary and Joseph!

Chorus 2: We don't care!

Chorus 1: Knock, knock!

Chorus 2: Who's there?

Chorus 1: Mary and Joseph!

Chorus 2: We don't care!

Chorus 1: Knock, knock!

Chorus 2: Who's there?

Chorus 1: Mary and Joseph!

Chorus 2: We don't care!

Chorus 1: Knock, knock!

Chorus 2: Who's there?

Chorus 1: Mary and Joseph!

Innkeeper: Well, I'll care! If you're not fussy, you can sleep in my cattle shed.

Narrator: So they did. Even a cattle shed is better than nothing when you are tired and God's son is going to be born at any moment. (*All exit.*)

Scene 3

Angels tell the shepherds about the baby.

Speaking: *Narrator, up to eight shepherds, angel, choruses 1 and 2*

Acting: *Shepherds, angel*

(*Shepherds enter and sit, as if around a fire.*)

Narrator: Out in the fields above Bethlehem, some shepherds were looking after their sheep.

Shepherd 1: It's cold tonight.

Shepherd 2: I'm tired.

Shepherd 3: Let's play a game to help us stay awake.

Shepherd 4: I know – I spy! I spy with my little eye, something beginning with 'A'. (*Angel enters.*)

Shepherd 5: (*Seeing the angel.*) Aaagh!!!

Shepherd 4: Wrong.

Shepherd 6: (*Seeing the angel.*) Aaagh!!!

Shepherd 4: No, I've said that's wrong!

Shepherd 7: (*Seeing the angel.*) Aaagh!!! Angel!!

Shepherd 4: No, it's not angel.

Shepherd 8: Yes it is!

Angel: Don't be afraid.

Shepherds: (*Seeing the angel.*) Aaagh!!!

Angel: I've got good news for you that will make everyone happy. God's son has been born in Bethlehem, and you'll find him lying on a bed of hay. (*Angels enter.*)

Chorus 1: Glory to God!

Chorus 2: Glory to God!

Chorus: Glory to God in heaven!

Chorus 1: Peace on earth!

Chorus 2: Peace on earth!

Chorus: Peace to God's people on earth!

Narrator: Then the angels left (*Angels exit.*), and the shepherds began to talk about what they should do.

Shepherd 1: Let's go and see!

Shepherd 2: Let's take a present!

Shepherd 3: Let's go now!

Shepherd 4: Come on!

Shepherds: Let's go! (*All exit.*)

Scene 4

The shepherds go to the stable to visit the baby.

Speaking: *Narrator, up to eight shepherds, Mary, Joseph*

Acting: *Shepherds, Mary, Joseph*

(Mary and Joseph enter and sit down. Then shepherds enter.)

Narrator: When the shepherds found the stable in Bethlehem, it was just as the angel had said.

Shepherd 1: There's the father!

Shepherd 2: There's the mother!

Shepherd 3: There's the hay!

Shepherd 4: But where's the baby?

Mary: He's here – asleep in my arms!

Shepherd 5: We were told about him by the angels.

Shepherd 6: They said he's God's son!

Shepherd 7: Is it true?

Joseph: Yes, it is. Jesus is God's son!

Mary: Would you like to look at him?

Shepherd 8: We've brought him a present.

Shepherd 1: It's not much – just a toy woolly lamb.

Shepherd 2: But it comes with our love.

Mary: Thank you very much.

Joseph: Thank you for coming.

Shepherds: Goodbye! *(They start to walk away.)*

Shepherd 3: Let's tell everyone we meet!

Shepherds: God's son is born! God's son is born! God's son is born! God's son is born! *(All exit.)*

Scene 5

The wise men come to worship Jesus.

Speaking: *Narrator, three wise men, Herod, Advisor*

Acting: *wise men, Herod, Advisor, Mary, Joseph*

(Enter wise men.)

Narrator: In a far country, wise men were studying the sky and saw a new star.

Wise man 1: It must be something very special – it's very bright.

Wise man 2: It must be something very special – it's very big.

Wise man 3: So it must mean something special.

Wise man 1: Let's look in our books! *(Mime.)*

Wise man 2: That's it! A new king, whose birth will be shown by the brightest star ever seen!

Wise man 3: So why are we just standing here looking at it – let's go and find him! *(All set off to walk.)*

Narrator: The star led them to Jerusalem, where they asked at the king's palace. *(Enter Herod and Advisor.)*

Herod: A new king of the Jews, you say? But it can't be true – I'm king here!

Wise man 1: That's what the star tells us!

Herod: I want to know more – what do my advisors say?

Advisor: The Messiah – God's special one – will be born in Bethlehem.

Wise man 2: Then we'll go to Bethlehem!

Herod: Well go and find him, and when you have done so, come back and tell me, so that I can worship him too.

Narrator: The wise men left Herod, but they never went back to him. God warned them in a dream that Herod wanted to harm the child. *(Exit Herod and Advisor.)* They went to Bethlehem, where they found the baby with his parents. When they saw him, they knelt down to worship him and to give him special gifts.

Wise man 3: I bring you myrrh – for though young now, one day you must die.

Wise man 2: I bring you frankincense, a gift for God's son.

Wise man 1: I bring you gold, a gift for a king.

Narrator: With that, the travellers returned to their home country *(Wise men exit.)*, leaving Mary and Joseph to care for the precious child, the son of God.

Scene 6

Why it happened and what it means.

Speaking: *Three Narrators, three voices*

Acting: *God, Jesus, Mary, Joseph, boy, girl, lots of people*

Narrator 1: But what is it all about?

Narrator 2: Long, long ago, when God first made the world, he enjoyed the friendship of the first people he had created. *(Two boys, one girl stand in a circle, all hands joined.)* He wanted only the best for them, and this friendship helped them to know how to live. But they chose to disobey God, and they spoiled and broke the friendship with God. *(Boy and girl drop hands and walk away from God.)*

Narrator 3: For many, many years God tried to help people to see how much he loved them, and that friendship with him was the best thing for them. But nothing changed. Something very special was needed to show them his love. And that very special something *(Mary and Joseph enter.)* was a tiny baby, God's son, whose coming would change the world.

Narrator 2: Joseph, who loved Jesus like his own son *(Jesus enters.)*, would have taught Jesus his trade of carpentry. And Jesus would have learned to love wood and to bend it to his will, to mend what had been broken and to make new things.

Narrator 3: When Jesus grew to be a man he left his family *(Jesus etc mime what is narrated.)* and travelled the country, telling people about God's love, making ill people better and doing wonderful things to help those in need. And as the angels had sung, there was glory to God through what Jesus did, and peace to those who met him and followed him.

Narrator 2: But not everyone liked him. Remember King Herod, who had wanted to kill the baby Jesus? and the gifts given to Jesus when he was born? Now, some people wanted to kill Jesus. And they did. Over his head they put a sign 'The King of the Jews'.

Voice 1: Gold, a gift for a king!

Narrator 2: Jesus let his body be shaped and nailed to a wooden cross, and he died.

Voice 2: Myrrh, a gift for one who must die.

Narrator 2: And as Jesus stretched out his hands on the wooden cross, he stretched out love from God to people, and the broken friendship was finally mended. *(Jesus stands facing audience, one hand out to God and one to man and woman, forming a cross.)*

Voice 3: Frankincense, a gift for God's son.

Narrator 3: But it couldn't end there – and it doesn't! Jesus came alive again, *(Jesus stands up straight.)* and he lives today to tell you how much God loves you.

Narrator 1: So this Christmas, remember God's love as you celebrate the birth of Jesus.

Narrators: Because that's what it's all about!!

Christmas craft – contents

Where to find all the craft in this book!

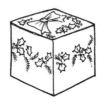

Christmas craft – contents

Mobile

stick

JESUS

longer
string
to
balance
only one
figure

Photocopy these
pictures onto
acetate, cut them
out and colour
them in with OHP
pens to make an
extra special
Christmas mobile.

Craft

Advent wreath

How to make your Advent wreath

The traditional Advent crown or wreath is made from a circle of evergreen leaves and branches to symbolise the never-ending nature of God's love. Sometimes people also add a few gold decorations to give the wreath a crown-like appearance and to emphasise Jesus' kingship.

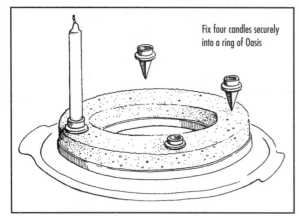

Fix four candles securely into a ring of Oasis

One candle is lit on the first Sunday of Advent, two on the second, three on the third and four on the fourth. The last candle, which is often larger and placed in the centre of the ring, can be lit on Christmas Day itself. The candles represent the light of God coming into the dark world. Week by week the candle light grows brighter as we come closer to Christmas.

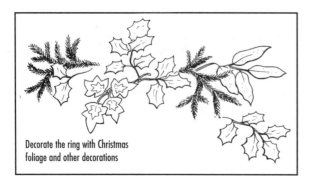

Decorate the ring with Christmas foliage and other decorations

Each week as the candles are lit, invite someone to read a relevant verse from the Bible and ask someone to say a short prayer. You might like to use some of the following verses:

Psalm 27:1
Isaiah 2:3–5
Isaiah 9:2,3
Isaiah 60:19,20
John 1:1–5
John 1:6–9

Choose one of these readings for Christmas Day: Luke 2:8–12 or Luke 2:28–32.

Each week sing an appropriate song such as 'Shine, Jesus, shine' or 'Shine bright, dazzle, dazzle'.

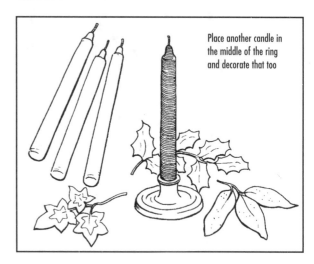

Place another candle in the middle of the ring and decorate that too

Your finished Advent wreath

How to make your banner

You will need: *a large piece of paper per banner (a length of wallpaper is ideal); felt-tip pens and other colouring equipment; collage materials; glue; length of garden cane or dowelling; string; sticky tape; clean-up and cover-up facilities*

Choose a simple design – one of the ones on this page or one of your own – and draw the outline on the paper (you may want the children to help you with this). Leave enough space at the top of the paper so you can hang the banner up when it is finished. Draw the words in outline, so the children can colour them in.

Draw the words in outline letters so the children can colour them in. Use simple Christmas shapes like stars and holly leaves to make striking designs and patterns. Give each child a shape to decorate or encourage them to use their shape to write a one-line prayer.

When the children have finished and the banner is dry, turn the paper over. Place the cane or dowelling near the top of the back of the banner and pull the top of the paper over it. Secure with sticky tape. Tie an end of a piece of string to each end of the cane or dowelling and hang your banner where it can be seen by everyone!

Finger puppets

Use these puppets with the story on page 60. The bold title at the beginning of each paragraph lists the puppets that you will need for each scene. You will need to make several angels and shepherds. Colour each one in a different way to give it an individual character.

When you glue the tabs in place, make sure that the name is still visible, that way you'll know which finger to move for each character, even though you can only see the back of your hand!

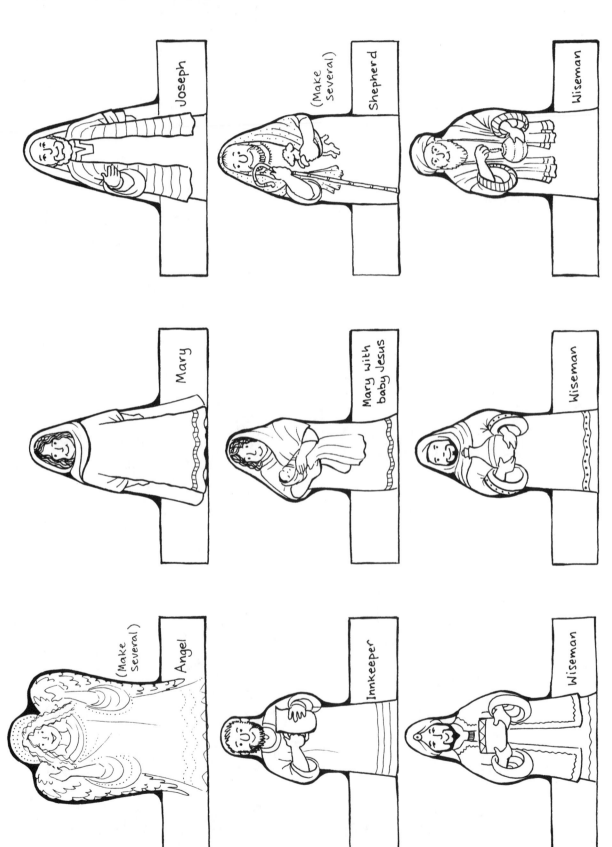

Craft

47

49

Make your own nativity scene

Make your own nativity scene

The nativity figures on these two pages have been designed to wrap around sections of kitchen roll tube. Cut out the characters and give them to individual children to colour in. If you have a large group, make several angels, shepherds and kings. Once the characters have been coloured, stick them to sections of kitchen roll tube to make instant stand-up figures. Some of the characters are taller than others, so it's a good idea to measure your cardboard tubes before cutting them. To complete the scene, colour a box brown and cover it with straw to make a simple stable. Add a circlet of tinsel to the top of the angels and a spot of cotton wool to the beards of the men for a pleasing effect.

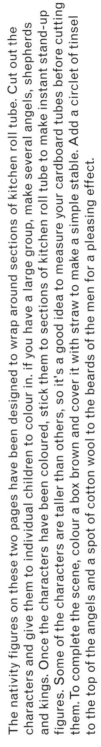

Craft

Blow-out angels

How to make a blow-out angel.

You will need:
two copies of the angel template,
wide drinking straws, narrow curling
gold ribbon, adhesive tape, crayons,
glitter, adhesive, scissors.

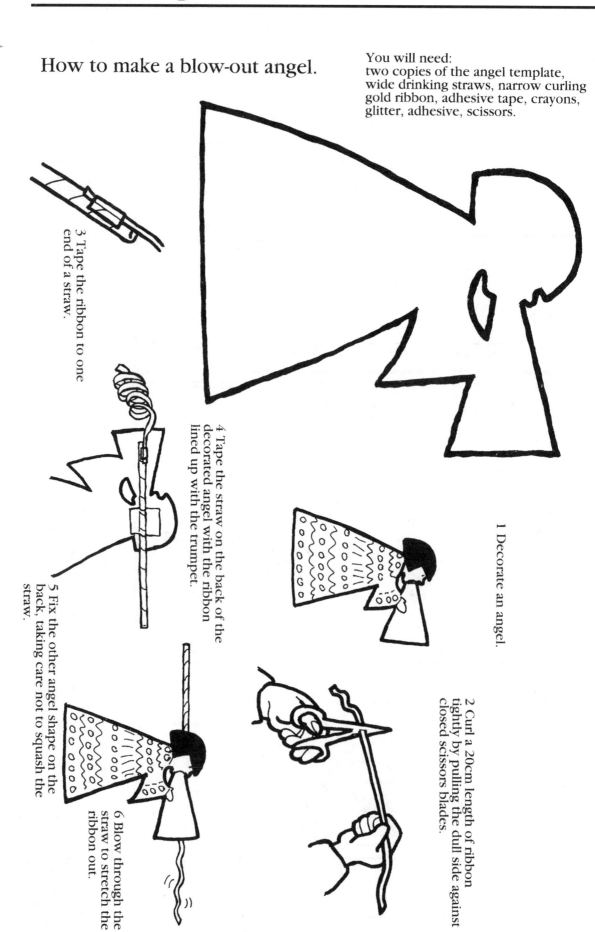

3 Tape the ribbon to one end of a straw.

4 Tape the straw on the back of the decorated angel with the ribbon lined up with the trumpet.

5 Fix the other angel shape on the back, taking care not to squash the straw.

6 Blow through the straw to stretch the ribbon out.

1 Decorate an angel.

2 Curl a 20cm length of ribbon tightly by pulling the dull side against closed scissors blades.

1.
Copy the shape on stiff white paper or thin card. Cut out circle & then along dotted lines...

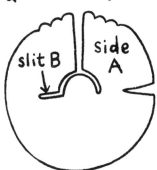

2.
With head facing forward pass side A behind the head & slip the slit onto slit B...

3.
An angel!

Craft

53

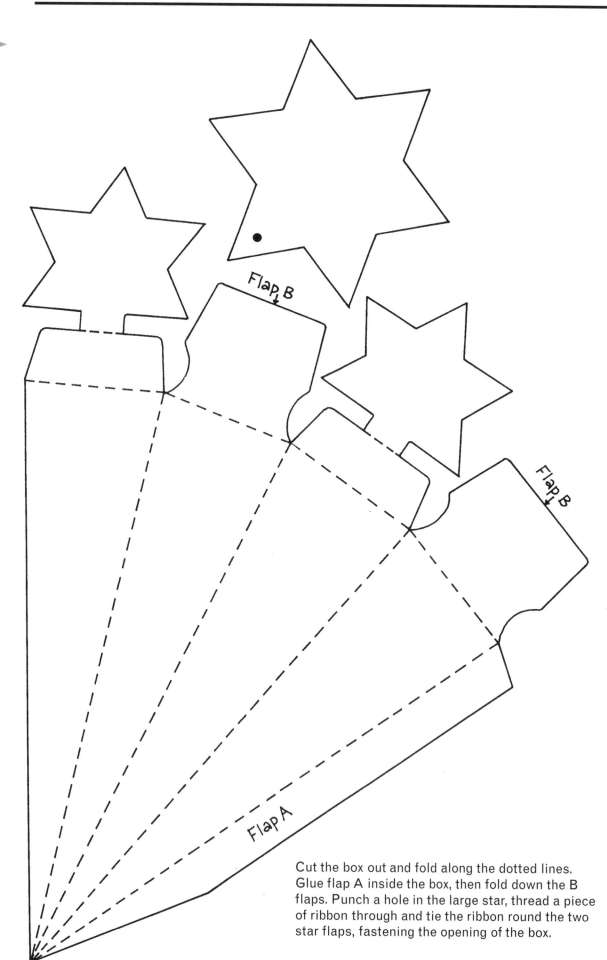

Flap B

Flap B

Flap A

Cut the box out and fold along the dotted lines. Glue flap A inside the box, then fold down the B flaps. Punch a hole in the large star, thread a piece of ribbon through and tie the ribbon round the two star flaps, fastening the opening of the box.

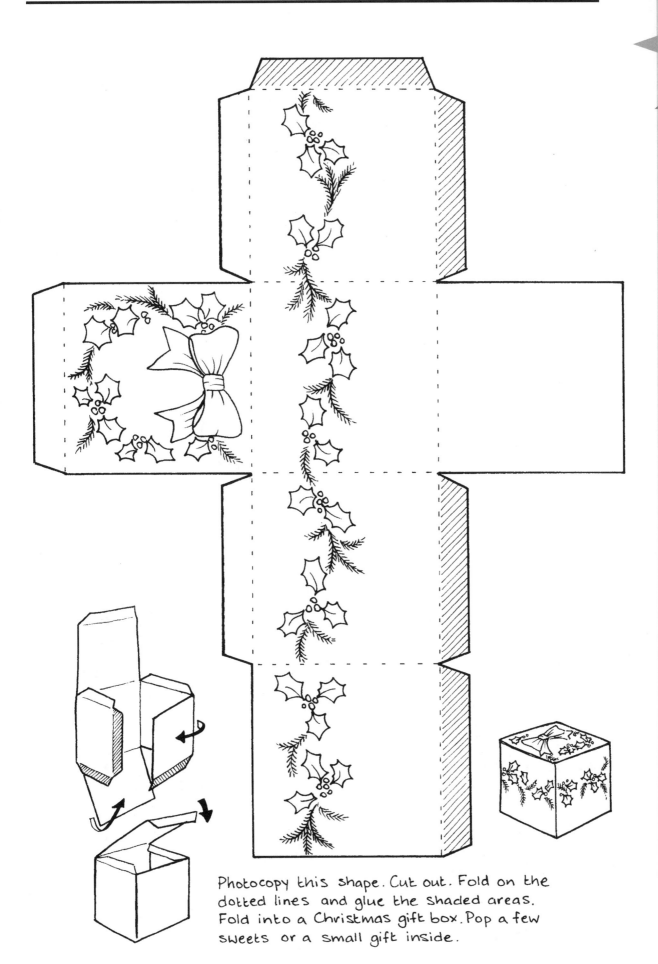

Photocopy this shape. Cut out. Fold on the dotted lines and glue the shaded areas. Fold into a Christmas gift box. Pop a few sweets or a small gift inside.

Christmas gift box

Craft

55

Pop-up angel card

Fold between arrows

▷ Colour and cut out the angel.
▷ Fold in half between the arrows so the arms point away from you.
▷ Fold feet forwards along dotted lines.
▷ Decorate the front of the card and write ' The angel's message about Jesus is true today.'

▷ Stand angel across the fold in the inside of the card with the feet at an angle, so the fold of the card aligns with the fold of the angel.
▷ Make sure the card will close with the angel folded and tucked away inside before sticking foot tabs down.

1 Take a rectangle of thin card and draw a simple picture on the front.

2 Carefully cut around the outline of the top half of the picture. Fold the top half back to make the card stand up.

3 Add your message on the front and inside.

4 Use the same method to make a variety of cards.

Overleaf you will find two fold up Christmas cards. Photocopy one sheet for each child in your group. Encourage the children to colour them in and perhaps add a sprinkling of glitter in the sky to look like stars. Fold the picture in four, keeping the artwork on the outside all the time, to make an attractive Christmas card.

This card was coloured especially for you by

'So they hurried off and found Mary and Joseph and saw the baby who was lying in the manger'

Luke 2:16

To...

Happy Christmas!

From...

From

HAPPY CHRISTMAS!

To

Wise men still seek him!

Matthew 2:2

Where is the child born to be
king of the Jews? We saw his
star in the east and have
come to worship him.

Finger puppet nativity story

An outline story by Judith Merrell that can be used with the finger puppets on page 46

An angel visits Mary

In the town of Nazareth lived a young girl called Mary. She was cheerful, kind and helpful. She lived at home with her mum and dad and helped about the house with cooking and fetching water, preparing food and looking after the animals. Mary was really looking forward to getting married to her fiancé, Joseph. One day when Mary was daydreaming about her wedding, a special visitor came to see her. Mary looked up from her housework and was amazed to see a bright, shining angel standing in front of her. She felt a bit frightened and started to tremble.

'Don't be afraid!' said the angel. 'I have a special message for you from God. God has chosen you to be the mother of his son. His name will be Jesus and he will be the king of all God's people.'

Mary was totally amazed, she could hardly believe her ears and she really couldn't think what to say.

'But... but... how can this be?' she asked. 'I... err... I'm not married yet.'

'Everything will happen through the power of God,' replied the angel. 'Nothing is impossible for him.'

Joseph sees an angel in a dream

Joseph was worried. He really loved Mary very much and he had been looking forward to marrying her, but now he had heard that she was going to have a baby and it wasn't his baby. That night Joseph tossed and turned in his sleep, as he wondered whether to stop the wedding. In his dreams an angel spoke to him.

'Don't break off your engagement to Mary,' the angel said. 'She loves you and she hasn't done anything wrong. God has chosen her to be the mother of his son. Go ahead and marry her and call the baby Jesus.'

When Joseph woke up he felt as if a weight had been lifted from him. He knew Mary still loved him and that God wanted him to marry her.

Mary and Joseph travel to Bethlehem and meet a kind innkeeper

One day Joseph and Mary set off for far-away Bethlehem, because the Emperor Augustus had decided that he wanted to know exactly how many people lived in his kingdom. Augustus ordered everyone to return to their original hometown so that he could count them all. Poor Mary was going to have her baby really soon so she could only walk very slowly. When the young couple finally arrived in the little town of Bethlehem there wasn't a single room left anywhere. They knocked on doors all over town but everyone said, 'Sorry, we're completely full up.' Then Joseph knocked on one last door.

'Sorry!' said the innkeeper, 'no room at all!' Then he looked at Mary and realised how tired and heavily pregnant she was. 'Well, I suppose there is the stable round the back. It's not very clean, but it is warm and dry – you can stay there if you like.'

That night Mary gave birth to Jesus and, because she didn't have a crib for him, she wrapped him up and laid him on a bed of hay in an animals' feeding trough.

Some shepherds receive a message from an angel and hear an angelic choir

Out in the fields, close to Bethlehem, a group of shepherds were watching over their sheep. Suddenly a bright light lit up the darkness. It was an angel, a messenger from God. The shepherds could feel their knees knocking. They had never seen a real angel before.

'Don't be frightened,' said the angel. 'I've got some really happy news for you. Today, in Bethlehem, a baby has been born. He is God's own special son.'

Suddenly, the sky was full of angels, all singing and praising God joyfully. The shepherds could hardly believe their eyes and ears.

The shepherds visit Joseph, Mary and Jesus

When the angels had gone back to heaven, the shepherds rushed off to Bethlehem to find the baby that the angel had told them about. Eventually they found the stable with Mary and Joseph and baby Jesus. Everything was just as the angel had described. They told the new parents all about their visit from the angels. Later they returned to their sheep, telling everyone that they met the good news about this new and very special baby.

Wise men visit Joseph, Mary and Jesus

Some time later some wise men from the east saw a new star in the sky. They knew that it was a special sign that a new king had been born. They travelled many miles to find Jesus, bringing him special gifts of gold, frankincense and myrrh because they realised that he was indeed someone very important. When they found Jesus, with his mother Mary, they knelt down and worshipped him.

Stories

60

A foxy tail

A short story by Geoffrey Grimes

We have a little farm. Just a few sheep, ducks and chickens. We store hay for our sheep in a barn. Some weeks ago my wife, Judy, went into the barn and saw a fox, standing on the hay bales. She just stood there, staring at Judy and then she walked slowly out of the big doors and up to the lane. She did not seem worried and was in no hurry to move away.

Every day since then, the fox has been there, curled up in a nest that she has made in the hay. She watches everything we do, and if we get too close she climbs up to the top of the stack, her ears pricked, her nose sniffing the unfamiliar smells.

On wet winter days I work in the barn, repairing things, and getting ready for the summer. Recently, I was in the barn painting some gates. To my surprise the fox lay on the hay watching me. She did not seem to be frightened by the noise I was making, or the smell of the paint that I was using.

After a long time she got up, stretched, and walked past me, so close that I was able to see, for the first time, that she was not well. Her fur was falling out and she was very thin. One of her ears even looked as though it had been chewed.

So I fetched some bread and milk and put it in a little dish near the place where the fox usually lay. Later I went back. She was there, but she hadn't touched the food. I tried to move the bowl nearer but she climbed up the hay stack to the top and stared at me warily.

What could I do? Was she wounded? She could not tell me how she felt. I could not explain that everything that I was trying to do was for her own good – that unless she accepted my help she would die.

Then I thought: if only I were a fox. I could speak to her in a language she could understand. She could tell me what was wrong. She would not be afraid of me. I could persuade her to eat something, before she became too weak...

It was at that moment that I thought of Christmas. Of course! That was why God became a human being – so that he could speak to us in our own language, so that we would not be frightened of him, so that he could explain to us how we can be made better. We are like that little fox, damaged by what we call sin – that is, not living the way God planned for us.

To help my little fox there would be no point in me simply becoming a fox, because then I would only have a fox's understanding. The two of us would be no better off. We would just be two little foxes together and I wouldn't be able to help her. No, to bring the help of humans to the sick fox, it would be necessary for me to become a fox/man. Then I could tell the sick fox what humans are like, what they think about and why they sometimes get angry with little foxes! It's the same with Jesus. If he had been just a human, he would not have been able to tell us about God. So although he was a complete human being, he remained fully God, and was able to tell us what God is like, how God loves us, and how he wants us to live our lives so that we will not go on hurting ourselves and each other. We could not have known any of these things, unless God had become a human being like us on that first Christmas.

Fortunately, my little fox overcame her fear and began to take some food. Slowly, she became stronger and her fur began to shine in the sunlight. She came less often for her food, until one day, she did not come at all. It seemed that God had not only taught us a lesson, but he had healed a little fox as well. Judy and I said a big 'thank you' to God, for both these things.

Feysal plays football

A short story by Rachel Coupe

Here is a story about a boy called Feysal. Although this is a 'made-up' story, there are many children living in our country who are just like him. Feysal and his family are refugees. That means that they have had to run away from their home because it is dangerous for them to stay there. Our story starts in a country called Somalia on the east side of Africa. One terrifying day, soldiers in heavy armour tanks drove into Feysal's village. Feysal had to hide inside a very small cupboard in the kitchen. It was dark in the cupboard and he couldn't see anything, but he could hear the soldiers firing with their guns at the house. When they had gone Feysal climbed out of the cupboard and looked at the holes the bullets had made in the walls of his house. He put his fingers into the round bullet holes and he felt very afraid.

After a very long journey, he and his family came to Britain as refugees, needing a new home where they could live and feel safe. Listen carefully to his story. Feysal is seven years old. It is nearly Christmas and it's his first day at a new school.

'Ouch! That hurt!'

The other boys were playing football in the playground. Woosh! The ball came flying over towards me and hit me on the ear. It really hurt! I wanted to cry – but I didn't. I didn't want the boys to see me cry because I wanted them to like me. I love football but nobody had asked me to play. I couldn't speak any English and I didn't understand a word they were saying. So at playtime I just stood in the corner of the playground while all the other children ignored me or gave me funny looks. I just stood there out in the cold, watching all the other children having fun and wishing that I could play football with the other boys.

I was very glad to hear the whistle blow and stood right at the end of the long line of children ready to walk back into the nice warm classroom. We marched into school, past the enormous glittering Christmas tree with red, flashing lights. It looked beautiful and was covered with bright shiny balls in different colours. I love balls so I reached out and touched a blue one gently. It was soft and smooth.

A teacher shouted at me very loudly, making me jump and wish that I was back at home with my mum and little sister Amina. I did not like this new school!

'Mum,' I asked, when we got home to our small, cold flat, 'can I go outside and play football?'

'No,' she said. 'I want you to stay inside the flat where you can be nice and safe with me.'

Mum finished locking the door. She had two keys and stretched up high to pull the bolt across the door at the top. Then she bent down low and pulled the bolt across the door at the bottom. I wish that Dad was here with us. I'm sure that he would have gone outside to play football with me! Mum saw the disappointed look on my face and said cheerfully, 'Don't be sad! You've had an invitation to go to a party tomorrow. I'm sure that there will be lots of games to play at the party.'

A party! I love parties. This was a special one organised by the local Christians for refugees who had needed to leave their homes like me. I couldn't wait to go!

The next day we arrived at the party in the church hall. You should have seen all the food! It all looked so strange and so colourful. I ate some crisps, salty and crunchy and scratching my throat as I swallowed. I liked the chocolate fingers better, and the chocolate melted all over my fingers making them brown and sticky. The red jelly wobbled and made me laugh and the ice cream quickly melted all over it to make a gooey, creamy sauce. There was the biggest cake I had ever seen, all covered in bright green icing and funny letters. Everywhere I looked there were balloons. (Amina played with a yellow one, but it popped loudly and made her cry.) We put on silly hats and played funny games, running backwards and forwards across the wooden floor. I laughed and laughed until my tummy hurt. It has been a long, long time since I laughed like that.

There were lots of other refugee children like me at the party. Mustafa came from my country, Somalia, and we quickly became friends. We had a competition to see who could eat the most chocolate fingers and we won first prize in the wheelbarrow race. Then we got told off for splashing about with water and making the floor wet. At last I had a friend that I could play with! Mustafa had been in England a lot longer than me, so he already knew how to speak English. He said that he was very lonely at first in his new school, but he has lots of friends now. I told him about the boys who played football at my school and how I really wished that I could play with them instead of just standing in the playground all on my own.

'Why don't you ask them if you can play too?' asked Mustafa.

'I can't,' I explained. 'I don't speak English.'

'It's easy,' said Mustafa. 'All you have to do is use sign language. Point to the ball and then point to yourself.' Mustafa made it sound very easy, but I still wasn't sure. 'Let's ask the church people if we can play football now,' he suggested.

He asked a friendly looking grown-up who answered in English. I didn't understand his words, but then he tapped his watch and pointed to a puppet theatre. I guessed he was saying that we could play football later, after the puppets, so I sat down on the carpet to watch the show.

The first puppet was a funny brown boy-figure with long dangly legs and hands that were pushed about with a long thin wire. It had a big red mouth and red socks. It was cool! The puppet introduced a play about the baby Jesus. My favourite part was when the three wise men went to the wrong place and ended up at King Herod's palace instead of the stable where Jesus was. King Herod was very funny. He went mad when he heard that they were looking for a new king. He jumped up and down, huffed and puffed, yelled and shouted. What a temper! His silly string hair kept getting stuck over his face as he tried to look angry (but it just made us all laugh). He changed his voice when he talked to the wise men, pretending that he was happy to hear that there would soon be a new King to take away his throne. As soon as the wise men had left the palace he was jumping up and down, ranting and raving again. One of the puppet wise men dropped his present for Jesus on the floor in front of the puppet theatre. That made us all laugh too! Then Joseph had a dream and an angel told him to escape to Egypt before King Herod could come and kill the baby Jesus. We didn't laugh then because we knew what it was like to have to run away from threats of death. Every child in that room watched in silence as the baby Jesus became a refugee, just like us. As the curtains closed we listened quietly to the sound of the donkey's plodding hooves, slowly making its way to Egypt.

A moments' silence, then I remembered that it was time to play football! The church leader played with us and he was very kind when Mustafa explained to him about my problem at school. He let me practise pointing to the ball and pointing to myself, then he ruffled my hair and gave me a wink.

'Go for it!' yelled Mustafa as we left the party. Clutching tightly hold of a blue balloon and a party bag with a piece of the bright green cake inside it, I started to think. I was quite looking forward to going back to school on Monday and trying out some sign language. I was sure that on Monday I would be able to play football in the school playground.

Monday came and I walked into the school entrance hall with the enormous, glittering Christmas tree. The red lights were still flashing, but this time I didn't touch the shiny balls and nobody shouted at me. Next to the tree stood Peter, another boy in my class. He was standing there holding a football in his arms. I pointed to the football and then I pointed to myself. Peter nodded and I knew he was going to let me play! I couldn't wait for playtime!

The morning's lessons seemed very long, but at last the bell rang for playtime. I looked across the room at Peter. Peter beckoned to me with his finger and led the way out to the playground.

The other boys were bigger and stronger than me so I tried really, really hard to play my very best. There were two bricks marking out the goal area and I was determined to score a goal. I ran really fast, but slipped over and hurt my knee.

'Are you OK?' asked Peter, pointing to my scratched knee. I smiled and shrugged my shoulders. I didn't need a plaster. Nothing was going to stop me from getting that goal. A kick here. A tackle there. The other team scored, but I didn't give up. I kicked the ball towards the goal. Would it score? No, not this time – but it was really close. Out of the corner of my eye I could see the teacher walking onto the playground with a whistle in her mouth. Not much time left now! The ball came in my direction. I kicked. The whistle blew. The ball flew between the bricks. I'd scored!

This time I lined up with the other boys slapping me on the back saying that I had been 'the man of the match'.

I love football.

I love my new school.

But most of all, I love my new friends!

Shepherds' surprise

A short story by Marjory Francis, for use with a parachute

Gather the children around the parachute and practise some of the actions that come later, without giving away where they come in the story. Tell the story as dramatically as you can, using the suggested actions given in italics.

The shepherds were sitting on the hillside at night. In the distance a wolf howled *(Howl like wolf.)*, but otherwise all was quiet and calm. *(Move the parachute gently up and down.)* Suddenly *(Throw the parachute up in the air.)* there was a bright light! An angel appeared! The shepherds were terrified and began to shake. *(Shake parachute.)* 'Don't he afraid,' said the angel. 'I have good news, which will be for everyone. This day, in Bethlehem, the city of David, a baby has been born. He is Christ the Lord! You will find him wrapped up in cloths and lying in an animals' manger.' *(As the angel speaks, make the parachute go up and down with strong powerful movements.)*

Then lots of angels appeared singing praises to God: 'Glory to God in the highest, and peace to his people on earth!' *(Repeat these words together while making a 'Mexican wave' around the parachute.)* When the angels had gone everything seemed quiet and still. *(Still the parachute.)* The shepherds decided to go to Bethlehem. They found the stable and crept inside. *(Lower your voice and make a 'cave' by raising the parachute over your heads, down your backs and sitting on the edge.)* There was the baby in the manger. They were very quiet. They looked at his little crumpled face and his tiny hands, and they marvelled. How could this tiny baby be God's special person? But they knew he was because he was in a manger, just as the angel had said.

The shepherds crept out again. *(Come out of the 'cave'.)* But once they were outside, they all began to praise God! *(Throw the parachute high.)*

Ask the children to each think of some words of praise that the shepherds might have shouted. If you feel it would he helpful, give them suggestions, such as 'Praise God for sending Jesus!' or 'Thank you, Lord!'

Call out the children in age groups, and as you raise the parachute high, that particular group runs underneath shouting out their praise to God.

Christingle services

Three Christingle service outlines by Helen Franklin

The Christingle service celebrates the 'Christ-light'; it is a service that often appeals to families who would not come to church for a more formal service, especially to those with quite young children. It is therefore helpful to keep it short and simple.

The Christingle is an orange into which have been stuck four cocktail sticks, and on each of these are skewered sultanas or sweets. Around the centre of the orange is a red ribbon, and into a hole made in the top of the orange is put a candle.

> The orange represents the earth.
> The four cocktail sticks represent the four seasons (or north, south, east and west).
> The fruit/sweets represent the fruit of the earth.
> The ribbon represents the blood of Jesus – or the love of Jesus – 'like God giving the world a big hug', as one infant teacher describes it.
> The candle represents Jesus, the Light of the World.

The Christingle service began over 250 years ago in a Moravian church in Marienborn, Germany. The tradition has spread around the world and many churches in the UK now hold an annual Christingle service in aid of The Children's Society. See: www.the-childrens-society.org.uk

Preparation

There should be enough Christingles for everyone who comes – adults as well as children – to have one and to take it home afterwards. It takes quite a while to prepare all of these but is well worth the effort! It's not a job for one person – get lots to help with a production line!

It is important to have wet towels, buckets of water or sand placed around the church in case of accidents, and to keep movement to a minimum when the Christingles are lit. Make sure that you have a first-aider present.

In selecting music for the service choose carols that are well known and are understandable to younger children. If possible, include one that they will sing at school (eg 'It was on a starry night') so that it will be familiar to those who are not used to church. If you are going to sing a carol whilst the church lights are out and the

Christingles lit, choose one that is simple and can be sung without songbooks by everyone. For this reason it may need to be 'Away in a Manger'!

It is wonderful to set the mood with lots of tea lights or candles around the church, and minimal electric lighting, to give it that 'Ooh!' factor when children come in. Who in your church has a good rapport with children? Get them to be part of the welcoming team as families arrive.

Afterwards

It is well worth serving tea/coffee/squash and mince pies/buns to encourage people to stay and talk a little. Prime regulars to be brave and to talk to those whom they don't know!

Have a leaflet about services at the church around Christmas available to give to people.

Why not offer people a gospel to take home? Choose a modern version, in colour if possible, so that it looks attractive – maybe Matthew or Luke so that they have some Christmas narrative, or John if you are doing the 'light' outline.

Outline 1
Jesus, the Light of the world

You will need: *a Christingle; matches; a miniature Christingle, eg made from a satsuma, and using a re-lighting candle (it needs to be a small orange so that the candle is in proportion). They are available in party shops*

Bible base: John 1:5

Ask or explain what the different parts of the Christingle mean.

Talk about Jesus' life on earth using the small Christingle, lighting it as you talk about his birth. Describe how he was born as a baby (hence the small Christingle), what he did in adult life and what he taught people about God, why he was hated by the religious authorities and why/how they killed him. At this point, gently blow out the re-lighting candle.

Proclaim the words of John 1:5: 'The light keeps shining in the dark, and darkness has never put it out.' (The candle should have re-lit).

Talk about Jesus' resurrection and how he will always be the Light of the World because the darkness can never put out his light.

65

Christingle prayer

Lord Jesus,
  You are the light, which shines in the darkness.
    You are the light, which guides our feet.
  You are the light, which fills us with a warm glow.
You are the light, which illuminates our lives.
You are the light, which leads us to safety.
You are the light, which will shine for ever.
You are the light of the world and we
worship you.

(From New Ideas for Creative Prayer, *SU, ISBN 1 85999 589 6)*

Tip! Don't forget to extinguish the candle properly, but do think carefully about when and where you do this, so as not to spoil your talk!

Outline 2
God's gifts through Jesus

You will need: *a Christingle; matches; some small, wrapped presents that would be suitable for you to receive, and that can be opened during the service; three things to represent gold, frankincense and myrrh*

Bible base: Matthew 2:11; 1 John

Talk about your presents and get someone to open them. Are they appropriate for you? What do they say about you?

The story of Jesus's birth includes him being given some gifts – not perhaps the most suitable for a newborn baby. Talk about the gifts and what each represents – gold for a king, incense used in worship for the Son of God, myrrh to show that his death would be significant. Talk about what each gift tells us about Jesus.

Through Jesus, God gave the most amazing gift to us. Show the Christingle and ask/explain what each part means. In particular:

the world and fruits represent God's gift to us of life.
the candle represents his gift of light (you could expand on this a little as to what life would be like without light, and what it means that Jesus is the light).
the red ribbon represents love – talk about Jesus's life, death and resurrection, and how God showed love through Jesus.

Outline 3
God's love shown in Jesus

You will need: *a Christingle; matches; (optional) dressing-up clothes for Mary and Joseph, plus a baby doll*

Bible base: Genesis 1–3; John 3:16

This could be prefaced by a quick and fun multi-choice Christmas quiz, the last question of which would be 'Why do we have Christmas?' (Answers to include such options as 'Because there are good films on the TV in late December; because the shops are full of decorations; because the world was in a mess and God wanted to put things right'.)

Then assemble a Christingle, relating the different parts to what Christians believe about God as you tell this narrative:

Long, long ago God made the world a good place to live, full of good things to eat and to enjoy (the orange, sticks and fruit). He looked at it and said 'That's good!'

Then he made people to be like him, and to be his friends. He looked at them and said 'That's very good!'

God gave them so many wonderful things to eat, but told them that they must not eat the fruit of one special tree.

You know what happens when someone says 'Don't do that!'? We go and do it! 'Don't touch that, it's hot!' warns someone. But we touch it, just to see if it is hot! Well, that's exactly what these people did: they ate the fruit of the tree that they were told not to eat. And you know when you've done something wrong, you get that horrible feeling inside? Not a tummy-ache from eating something bad, but an ache because you know you've done something bad. Well, that's how it was for these people, because they had spoiled their friendship with God.

But God had decided to do something about it. He sent Jesus into the world to be the light of the world (put in candle) because God loved the world so much.

Jesus came as God in human form to love the world. He was born as a baby to Mary and Joseph, whom God had chosen to love and to look after his son. (If you want to dress up children or adults to be Mary and Joseph, bring them out now.) They had to travel to Bethlehem, which was the place where Joseph's family came from – not his father or grandfather, but perhaps his grandfather's grandfather, or his

grandfather's grandfather's grandfather – or even further back in time than that! And while they were staying in Bethlehem, Jesus was born.

Maybe when he grew older Jesus helped his earthly father with his carpenter's work, making furniture and tools for people. Until one day, when Jesus was a grown man, he knew that it was time to start doing his heavenly father's work. So he began to teach people what God was like, what God wanted them to be like, and he began to show people what God is like by loving them, caring for them and healing them.

Jesus did this most of all when he died on the cross, when he was punished for all the wrong things that everyone has ever done, and all the wrong things that you and I do, so that we could be friends for ever with God.

And just to make sure we knew that he'd put things right, God brought him alive again so that he would live for ever.

So the ribbon around the middle of the orange (put this in place) reminds us of God's love: the red is said to be like Jesus's blood as he died on the cross. Or, you might say, it's like God giving the world a big hug.

This Christmas, remember how much God loves you: that Jesus came to give you a big hug from his Father God. And have the happiest Christmas ever.

Christmas toddler/pram service

A service outline by Steve Hutchinson

This special toddler story time can be slotted into a normal parents and tots session. It takes about 15 to 20 minutes, depending on which activities you choose. After an opening free play session, take the children and their parents or carers into the church or to a corner of your room for a story and singing time as described below. After this story time, stop for refreshments and let the children go back to free play. At this point you might like to include a craft table and help the children to make one of the crafts suggested on pages 42 to 59, for example Instant angels on page 53.

Introduction

Explain that this week we are going to hear how Mary and Joseph had to walk a very long way. Round up the children and lead them to the story corner or church saying 'tramp, tramp, tramp' as you go. It's a very long way to Bethlehem – tramp, tramp, tramp. Invite everyone to sit down but keep on walking using fingers on floor/arm until all are settled and ready to listen.

Story, part one

Tell the story of Mary and Joseph travelling to Bethlehem and then looking for somewhere to stay. Go on to explain how Jesus was born in a stable at the back of an inn.

You might like to tell the story from a children's Bible. Alternatively use the finger puppets and story on pages 46 and 60. Finish the story with either the action rhyme or song below.

Action rhyme

This is the roof of the stable small
(Make roof shape with hands.)
This is the manger, the animals' stall
(Cup hands together.)
This is the baby, asleep on the hay
(Rock baby gently.)
God's gift to us on the first Christmas Day.
(Stretch hands out offering present.)

Or song

Sing the following words to the tune of 'The wheels on the bus go round and round':

Joseph and Mary went tramp, tramp, tramp,
Tramp, tramp, tramp! Tramp, tramp, tramp!
Joseph and Mary went tramp, tramp, tramp,
All day long.

Baby Jesus was born in Bethlehem,
Bethlehem, Bethlehem.

Baby Jesus was born in Bethlehem,
Long, long ago.

The angels in the sky sang, 'Glory to God!'
'Glory to God! Glory to God!'
The angels in the sky sang, 'Glory to God!'
All night long.

The sheep in the fields went, 'Baa, baa, baa!'
'Baa, baa, baa! Baa, baa, baa!'
The sheep in the fields went, 'Baa, baa, baa!'
All night long.

Joseph and Mary went, 'Shhh, shhh, shhh!'
'Shhh, shhh, shhh! Shhh, shhh, shhh!'
Joseph and Mary went, 'Shhh, shhh, shhh!'
All night long.

Tip! Have the words to all the songs, rhymes and prayers written on large cards or on an OHP acetate so that all the parents and carers can join in.

Searching game

Hide the following items in the church for the little ones to look for: a cuddly lamb, a baby doll, a manger, a star, a crown, something gold, frankincense (a scented candle or joss sticks), myrrh (some hand cream or body lotion).

Story, part two

Talk about these items and use them as visual aids as you tell the next part of the story in which the angels visit the shepherds and send them to see Jesus, and then some time later the wise men arrive. Use a children's Bible or tell the story in your own words.

Prayer

A leader can say the following prayer line by line for everyone to repeat:

Thank you for the baby
Who came on Christmas Day
Thank you it was Jesus,
Who came to earth to stay.
Thank you that you love us
And always will be near,
Thank you God for Christmas
This happy time of year.

OR

Use this response prayer with everyone joining in the words 'Thank you, God'.

At Christmas we say *Thank you, God*, for fun and games to play.
At Christmas we say *Thank you, God*, for special treats and lovely food.
At Christmas we say *Thank you, God*, for presents from our family and friends.
At Christmas we say *Thank you, God*, most of all for Jesus, born as a baby.

Final song

Sing the following words to the tune of 'Frere Jacques'.

Baby Jesus, baby Jesus
Lying in the hay, lying in the hay
Shepherds came to see him, shepherds came to see him
Wise men too, wise men too.

OR

Sing the following words to the tune of 'Polly put the kettle on'.

Praise to God in heaven, praise to God in heaven,
Praise to God in heaven, the angels sang.

Peace on earth to everyone, peace on earth to everyone,
Peace on earth to everyone, the angels sang.

by Rachael Champness from Let's sing and shout!*, published by SU, ISBN 1 85999 263 3*

> **Tip!** For more materials for under-fives check out the Tiddlywinks series of resource books, published by Scripture Union. The **Tiddlywinks Big Red Book** is particularly suitable for Christmas: ISBN 1 85999 658 2

Christmas toddler/pram service

Getting ready to welcome Jesus

An all-age Advent Sunday service by Ro Willoughby

Advent Sunday is a wonderful time to begin preparations for Christmas before all the Christmas festivities overwhelm us. This service was held on 1 December 2002. The following six principles were taken into consideration by those planning the service:

☆ Just one key teaching point
☆ Allowance made for the different ways in which people learn
☆ Active participation of all ages to be encouraged
☆ The concepts talked about to be child-friendly at all times although the language may sometimes be beyond the smallest children present
☆ Suitable for those present who are not regular church-goers
☆ Space for 'family news', recognising that the regulars are part of a church community.

Theme: Preparing to welcome Jesus into our lives.

Advent gives us time to think about Jesus' first coming, and how he will come as king a second time. But every day, we can welcome him into our lives. We will explore what it means to prepare for Jesus as we look at how Mary got ready for Jesus' birth.

You will need: *For every person present, an envelope in which is a paper-wrapped sweet, a piece of pipe-cleaner (half will do) and a small piece of sticky-back paper; a pen or pencil for everyone; a new mother or a pregnant woman who is prepared to be interviewed; a large board on which is written at the top the next year, eg 2004*

Welcome

Explain that this is a service for people of all ages as we begin to prepare for the coming of Jesus. People should feel free not to join in if they are uncomfortable. Thank God that he is with you all.

Song

A song of praise such as 'Praise my soul the king of heaven', known by the occasional church attender.

Game

Play 'Hide and Seek' ('Coming, whether you're ready or not!')

Brief the participants in advance.

Two children are given 20 seconds to hide in the church. Two or more children stand with their backs to the congregation. Everyone counts up to 20, then everyone calls out 'Coming, whether you're ready or not!' When the 'hiders' have been found, explain that the 'seekers' were not going to wait until the 'hiders' were ready. In the same way, lots of things happen whether we are ready or not – Christmas, exams, moving house. But it is much better if we are ready!

Family news

Share news of particular events for which there is some preparation needed! Talk about the preparation.

Interview

Invite a new mother or pregnant woman to talk about how she got ready for her baby, who came whether she was ready or not! In particular, ask the following:

What things is she getting for the baby?
How is she preparing herself for the baby, physically, emotionally and spiritually?
How does she look at the future now that there is a baby to think about?

Bible reading

Luke 1:26–45,56. This is a long reading so make sure it is read by good, well-prepared readers using a child-friendly version. A narrator with readers for the parts of the angel, Mary and Elizabeth would be a good way to split up the passage.

Entering the story

Mary prepared for Jesus, just like any new mother gets ready for her baby, except Jesus was a bit different. We'll be looking at what she did and letting that challenge how we also can prepare to welcome Jesus into our lives every day.

1 Mary thought about someone else

Having a baby for Mary was just like it is today but babies didn't need all the equipment that babies seem to need these days! (Refer to the interview!) But she was going on a journey just before Jesus was due so she probably took something to wrap the baby in to keep him warm. She didn't have to think of a name because the angel had told her that the baby would be a boy and would be called 'Jesus' (verse 31).

Activity

We can prepare for Jesus by thinking of others

Christmas is a time for giving and thinking of others. (Give out the envelopes but instruct people not to do anything with the three things inside until you say so.)

Invite each person to give a sweet to someone in the service who they want to say thank you to or show that they are cared for, eg thank a Sunday group leader or the person who welcomes people at the door or someone who has been ill.

Take up the offering and light the Advent candle if this is part of your practice.

2 Mary was preparing herself to be a mother
Soon after the angel had come to Mary, she went to visit her cousin, Elizabeth (verses 39,40). This was a long journey and she stayed there for about three months, maybe until after the birth of John the Baptist (verse 56). This would have given her practical experience of babies! Certainly, Elizabeth was an older, wise and godly woman who welcomed and supported Mary (verses 42–45). Refer back to the interview. Mary must have spent a lot of time thinking and talking with God about all that had happened. By the time Jesus was born she understood some fantastic things about God and what he had done for her. He had chosen her to be the mother of his son!

Activity

We can prepare for Jesus by thinking about and talking with God

Ask everyone to shape the pipe-cleaner into the shape of their initial. God knows each one of us by name and loves us personally. Invite each person to hold their pipe-cleaner. Play some quiet music for about 45 seconds while each person quietly thanks God that he knows each of us by name and loves us as we are.

Children's reading

From Luke 1:46–55. Younger children could read the following simplified version of Mary's song which comes from *Tiddlywinks: My Little Red Book*. Children can read the italicised lines. Everyone present can join in a second time.

Mary's song

Everything inside me wants to sing to you God.
Oh God, you are great!
You care for me even though I am
not important.

And people will now remember me forever, because I shall be the mother of Jesus.
Oh God, you are great!
You are so kind.
You care for people who are not strong, because you are so strong.
Oh God, you are great!
You care for people who are hungry.
You keep your promises.
Wow! You are so fantastic!
Oh God, you are great!

Song

Sing songs which allow space to acknowledge God's greatness. These might include 'Tell out my soul'; 'Lord of the future, Lord of the past'; 'Our God is a great big God'.

3 Mary was preparing for the future
Life was never the same again for Mary. She knew that her son would do great things. That must have been an amazing and a scary thought. But she knew that God was powerful and he was in control.

Activity

We can prepare for Jesus by asking him to be with us in the future

Ask everyone to write or draw something which they would like God to do for them in the new year. Give some suggestions. Invite people to stick their piece of paper on the big board at the front as a symbolic gesture.

Prayer

Pray for the future as we prepare for Jesus to come, now and at Christmas. Pray specifically for situations of uncertainty in the world and in your own community.

Finally...

Give information about the Christmas programme and thank everyone for participating.

Final song

Sing a song such as 'Over all the earth' or 'O come all you faithful'.

Tiddlywinks: My Little Red Book is published by Scripture Union, ISBN 1 85999 659 0.

Endings and beginnings

An all-age nativity service by Peter Graystone

This service has been devised to offer participation for children, rather than performance by children. The service follows the account of Jesus' birth in Matthew's Gospel, which describes the visit of the wise men to Bethlehem.

Preparation

One of the features of this service is spontaneity! It requires careful preparation, but it does not require children to rehearse, dress up or learn lines.

During the service, everyone hears the story contained in Matthew 2:1–12. Children are invited to take part in the service by acting out the roles of wise men and their servants. While carols are being sung by the rest of the congregation, they form a procession which moves around the church building representing the journey of the wise men from the east to Bethlehem and beyond. At each stage they return to the front of the church to make a discovery and hear the next part of the story. Obviously the carols can be changed to suit the tradition of the church, but the suggestions below have been chosen to fit the progress of the story and are particularly suitable for those who come to church only occasionally. In each case, only a selection of verses need to be sung.

You will need: *A number of children, who could be accompanied by parents and other adults if this is desirable, to form the procession;*

Something for each child in the procession to hold. Depending on the number of children in the church, these could include half-a-dozen cardboard crowns for the wise men (as we don't know how many there were), pretend or real candles in suitable holders or lanterns (obviously there are safety issues here, but older children may feel that their contribution has been more significant if their participation has required a higher level of responsibility than younger ones);

A large star, made of card, on the end of a pole and an adult to carry it;

Large copies of the text of five riddles;

Three 'gifts' of gold (perhaps a gold-coloured box), frankincense (a perfume jar with an interesting shape) and myrrh (possibly represented by a thorny branch);

Three adult actors, who could be costumed. One represents Herod, and sits on a grand chair. The other two represent Mary and Joseph, and carry either a doll or real baby to represent Jesus;

Two adults to move the 'props' during the carols;

And importantly, you need a really good narrator. A child or group of children honestly will not do – it has to be someone with the confidence to take control of what is going on, even if it is not happening quite as planned!

Welcome

May I give you a warm welcome and wish you a very happy Christmas! Today we have come together to hear in words and carols the timeless and true story of Jesus Christ, born on the first Christmas Day. We are going to follow the route taken by some important and learned men as they travelled to find the baby Jesus in a house in Bethlehem. We are going to act out one of the great journeys of human history, and I hope that our play will lead us all to worship Jesus the King, just as those wise men did two thousand years ago.

But where are the actors? Where's the scenery? Well, they are all here in the room with us, they just don't know it yet! In a moment, I am going to invite any boys and girls who would like to take part to accompany me on a procession that will lead us in our imaginations back through history to the town where Jesus was born. So come and join me at the front of the room if you are young or young at heart. Bring a grown-up with you if you would like their company on our journey, and find a seat on the floor in front of me as we all sing 'O come all you faithful'.

Carol

'O come all you faithful'. While this is being sung, children who wish to take part come to the front. Give some of them a crown, others candles or lanterns. Ask them to sit at your feet.

Narration

Our story begins in a far distant country, many miles away in the east. It is a tale of wisdom and learning; a tale of danger and bravery; a tale of worship and wonder. It concerns some very wise people studying at one of the ancient, oriental universities. You will see who they are on our procession because they are wearing crowns. And I am sure they were attended by faithful, helpful servants. You will see who they are because they will be lighting the way for our procession with their candles.

The wise men studied the stars in the sky, and they studied the writings of the generations that had gone before them. They may well have read or heard the magnificent stories of the Jewish race, God's own chosen people. Those stories told of the great King of the Jews, whom the people expected would come to lead them to freedom. And called him the Messiah, the great leader, whom God would send for the Jews and for the whole world. And surely it must have been God himself who revealed to them that the time was right for the Messiah to be born, because even though they had miles and miles to travel, they made up their minds that they would go and find this great man. So, just as ours is about to, their journey began.

But how did they know which way to go? And for that matter, how will we know which way to go? Well boys and girls, follow me and we will find the route together. And to help us know the way, here is a riddle which will tell us what we are looking for:

Wise men, look up at God's wonderful skies,
Wait till it's night-time and open your eyes;
What you are seeking is twinkling with light,
It will direct you the way that is right.

If you can solve that, you must be as wise as the wise men were! Boys and girls, we will set off on our journey to solve the riddle while everyone else sings 'Brightest and best of the sons of the morning'.

What did they take? We must go and find out! And the riddle that will help us is this:

Wise men, who search for the King of the Jews,
God has announced to the world his good news,
If you look hard you'll find presents to bring,
Fit for a prophet, a priest and a king.

Carol

'Brightest and best of the sons of the morning'. While the congregation is singing, the narrator leads the procession at a dignified pace up one side of the room, round the back of the congregation and down the other side so that everyone ends up back where they started. (Naturally, you can adapt the route to suit your setting.) This is repeated during each carol, so the journey (or a variation on the route) is made four times in all. On each occasion, while the children are walking, something new appears at the front of the room. On this occasion it is a large, shiny star held high in the air on a stick. Each time the children arrive back at the front, they sit down in front of their new discovery.

Narration

So that was the answer to the riddle. A star! High in the sky it shone, and the wise men were able to pick it out as quite different from any

other. It was by this star that they knew the time was right for God to do something new and marvellous in our world. And it was by this star that they knew they must travel to Jerusalem, the holiest city of the Jews. I am sure they imagined that such an important person as the Messiah would be born in a palace or a temple, and knowing they were to visit a king, they took something with which to greet him. What did they take? We must go and find out! And the riddle that will help us is this:

Wise men, who search for the King of the Jews,
God has announced to the world his good news,
If you look hard you'll find presents to bring,
Fit for a prophet, a priest and a king.

We've got two things to help us now! The riddle will show us what to search for and, look, the star is already moving to show us where to go. So I think we should follow it while everyone sings 'As with gladness men of old'.

Carol

'As with gladness men of old'. The person carrying the star leads the procession round the church, and when it returns to the front 'stage managers' have put in place three gifts representing gold, frankincense and myrrh.

Narration

What strange gifts to take a baby – gold, frankincense and myrrh! But the baby the wise men were to visit was no ordinary baby, and the gifts the wise men took were no ordinary gifts. Gold was a gift fit for a king. Frankincense was a perfume used in worship in the temple, and it was a gift fit for God himself. Myrrh was a sweet-smelling ointment used when people were terribly ill, and it was a gift fit for someone whose death would be remembered for ever. I think we should take them with us on our journey to find the Messiah, the King of the Jews. We know we are heading for Jerusalem; I wonder whether the riddle will help us know what to look for?

Wise men, your journey will lead to a palace,
When you get there you'll have a surprise,
You'll meet a king, he's not to be trusted,
Take his advice, but beware of his lies.

Well, it sounds as if our journey might take us to a dangerous place. Let's go and find out as everyone sings 'We three kings of Orient are'.

Carol

'We three kings of Orient are'. The procession moves on and arrives back to find King Herod sitting in pomp on a throne.

Narration

This is certainly a king, but it is not the King of the Jews for whom we are looking. And the riddle warned us not to trust him! His name is King Herod. When he found out that the wise men had arrived in his city, he grew upset. He heard that they were asking everyone, 'Where is the baby who will become King of the Jews?' He was very worried and angry at that, because he did not want another king to come and take his power away. So he found out from his religious advisors where the Jewish people expected the Messiah to be born. The answer came back: 'Ancient Jewish scriptures say he will be born in Bethlehem.'

When he heard this, Herod asked the wise men to pay him a visit, which is why we are sitting in front of him now. He pretended to be really kind to them. He said, 'I'm sure you will find the one you are looking for in Bethlehem. And when you find the right house, come back and tell me where it is so that I can go there and worship him too.' But he was telling a dreadful lie. He didn't mean to worship the baby; he meant to harm him! Now, wise men, what do you think we should do? Should we take horrid Herod with us to Bethlehem? (Shake your head and wait for a chorus of 'no'.) How wise you all are! Let's leave him and continue our journey. We know we are going to Bethlehem now. That's good! Perhaps this riddle will help us:

Wise men, don't search in a temple or palace,
Look for a house that is small, poor and sad,
God's way is not through the rich or powerful,
Search for a baby, his mum and his dad.

Oh wonderful! The star is on the move again. Doesn't that make you glad! Let's follow as we sing 'Unto us a boy is born'.

Carol

'Unto us a boy is born'. Following the star, lead the children to Mary, Joseph and Jesus (a toddler or doll). As you approach, indicate to the children to tiptoe so that there is a sense of awe at approaching the family.

Narration

A baby, his mum and his dad! That's what the riddle told us to look for, and here they are. The wise men entered the house where they were staying, and that is where they found Mary, Joseph and their young child whose name was Jesus. And when they saw Jesus, they knew their journey was at an end. They had found the baby who was born to be King of the Jews. They knew that they were in the presence of someone who had come from God and was quite unlike any other baby before or since.

So they knelt down in front of him, and they gave him their gifts. Let's all do that now! (Do so.)

It's right to worship Jesus, because he is the baby who grew to be the man who did everything it takes to allow God and humans to be friends. He was not only the Messiah, for whom the Jews waited, he was the Saviour of all the world. So as we kneel here, thinking how Jesus was sent from God to be born among us, let's sing a song of worship. Boys and girls, you can join in this one! It's 'Away in a manger'.

Children's song

'Away in a manger'.

Narration

And here is the final riddle:

Wise men, King Herod won't worship the baby,
He plans to kill him, whatever he says,
Don't tell him where he can find Lord Jesus,
Go back home by alternative ways.

Well, wise men, you've heard the riddle. Do you think we should go back and see Herod again? ('No!') Do you think we should go back to our homes instead? ('Yes!') That just shows how wise you have grown, because Herod did try to harm Jesus. He sent soldiers to kill him, but by the time they got to Mary and Joseph's house, they had already escaped and run away to the safety of Egypt. They didn't come back until King Herod had died and it was safe to do so. And Jesus grew up to be the most important person in the history of the world. Why? Because those who follow him as their friend and Lord will live the best life on earth and will live a perfect life in heaven. What a wonderful thing! Don't forget how special it is to know that in all the hurly-burly of Christmas this week.

Well, boys and girls, it's time for you to go and find the grown-ups with whom you came to church, just as the riddle told us. Do so while we sing 'O worship the Lord'.

Carol

'O worship the Lord in the beauty of holiness'. Children return to their places, keeping their crowns and candles as a souvenir.

Prayer

Lord God, as we celebrate Christmas this week, make us like the wise men, full of generosity, eager to worship Jesus, determined to do good. May our celebrations bring joy to those around us, and bring joy to you. Amen.

Final carol

'Once in royal David's city'.

Celebrate Christmas!

Preparation

This all-age nativity service has been devised to offer maximum involvement and minimum rehearsal. You will, however, need to do some advance preparation.

You will need: *a leader, up to six readers and up to eight prayer readers who will need to have scripts in advance. You will also need to appoint on the day at least 15 people of all ages who need no prior warning (see instructions below). The nativity story is told in the words of the Bible and uses props to make people think. A tableau of the characters is gradually arranged and a simple challenge is included at the end.*

Before the service, prepare a number of boxes wrapped as Christmas gifts. Each box should have a number on it and a label saying it is not to be opened until the designated time. Make sure the gifts can be opened quickly and easily. Wrap them as lavishly as possible, so that they look exciting.

Boxes 2, 5, 7, 9, 11, 13 and 15 should each contain a card with the number or title of a carol. (Make sure the 9 is not confused with a 6.) These should be written clearly and large enough to be held up and shown to the congregation. The contents of the other boxes are as follows:

1 A Bible
3 (to represent Isaiah) a telephone, toy or mobile
4 (Mary) an engagement ring (or a toy ring)
6 (Joseph) a tax form
8 (innkeeper) a sign saying 'no vacancies'
10 (shepherds) have several boxes with this number; each should contain a pair of sunglasses
12 (wise men) if possible, have three boxes with 12 on them; one should contain a horoscope page from a newspaper or magazine, another a map and the third a travel brochure
14 a plastic rubbish sack (wrap this in a heavy box, so that the box could appear to contain a doll).

These 'gifts' are given out as people come into church. You may want to warn those who will play the principal parts in advance. It is obviously necessary for a female to be Mary, and for males to play the parts of Isaiah, Joseph, at least some of the shepherds and the wise men. It might be more fun, however, to colour code the labels, eg red for females, blue for males and green for either, and offer them

An all-age nativity service by Marjory Francis

to anyone who is feeling brave as they come in. Choose a good mixture of adults and children. Tell them that they will be required to stay at their place and open the box when requested, and then take part as required.

You will need a central dais where you can set up the tableau with benches or stools, and something to represent a manger. You will also need a doll – keep it well out of sight until it is needed.

Choose an experienced leader who will make sure the pace of the service is not slowed down by the opening of the gifts.

There are six readings from the Bible. These need to be practised in advance. They could be read by one person from a central place (not the main leader), or by several different ones who stand up in their own place in the church. Although it might be tempting to have the readings printed out, to keep the integrity of the script it would be better to have them read directly from a Bible.

There is a section of prayers. These could be read by the leader, by two voices alternating, or divided up among a group.

Welcome

May I give you all a very warm welcome. We have come together today to hear the story of Jesus, the baby who was born on the first Christmas – Jesus, who is the Son of God. At Christmas, we all think a lot about presents – presents we might give and presents we might receive. Today, as you came into church, some of you were given a gift. Don't worry if you weren't given one, as they are for us all to share. They will be opened one by one through the service. If you have one of these gifts, please make sure you wait until you are asked to open it, then we can join in the excitement!

Could the person with gift number 1 stand up and hold up your gift? *(Number 1 stands and shows the gift. They are then asked to open it and show the contents [a Bible] to the congregation.)* This is a reminder that the story we are going to hear today is from the Bible. Throughout our service we will be listening to this true story as it was written down many years ago. *(Number 1 sits down.)*

Carol

Ask Number 2 to open their gift, which contains the title of an opening carol. *(The person opening*

the gift should read the card out and hold it up for the rest of the congregation to see. Suggested carols include 'O come, all you faithful'; 'Come on and celebrate'.)

Narration

Please could we open gift number 3 (a telephone). What do we use a telephone for? To communicate and send messages. Sometimes, when there's someone we particularly want to get hold of, we wish we had a hotline directly to them. All through the Bible there are messages from God, and many of them in the Old Testament are about God's Messiah, his special person who was coming. Isaiah was one of these prophets who seemed to have a hotline to God.

Reading Isaiah 9:2,6,7

Narration

So God has promised that his special person, the Messiah, the anointed one is coming. But how is this going to happen? Please could we open gift number 4 (*a ring*). It's a ring because this young girl named Mary (*Indicate the person who opened the 'gift'.*) is engaged to be married. (*If possible, 'Mary' should put the ring on her finger.*) But before Mary can get married, something very strange and wonderful happens. She has a visit from an angel!

Reading Luke 1:26–38

Narration

Mary finds she is pregnant – but she is not married! This was shocking, even punishable by death in those days. But the news is good, not bad as it would seem, because it is from God and this is no ordinary baby. As we think about this part of the story, let's open gift number 5.

Carol

Number 5 contains a carol. (*Suggested carols include 'Tell out my soul'; 'The angel Gabriel'.)*

Narration

Now for gift number 6. Let's open this one, please. A tax return. Most of us have had them, and so did Joseph here. (*Indicate the person who opened the 'gift'.*) Joseph is Mary's fiancé. He has had problems accepting the news about the baby, but an angel visited him too, and told him that it was all part of God's plan. Now, just as the baby's due, he's had a summons from the Roman tax office to go and register at Bethlehem, 70 miles away!

Reading Luke 2:1–7

Carol

Please could we open gift number 7. This contains the title of a carol. (*Suggested carols include 'O little town of Bethlehem'; 'Once in royal David's city'. During this carol, Joseph should collect Mary and bring her to the front of the church, where they remain standing.)*

Narration

What happened when Joseph and Mary arrived at Bethlehem? Let's open gift number 8 (a 'no vacancies' sign). There was no room for Mary and Joseph to stay. What would they do?

Reading Luke 2:5b–7

Carol

Please could our innkeeper come and show Mary and Joseph into the stable. As they settle in, let's open gift number 9. (*Indicate the dais area. The innkeeper should come forward and 'show them in'. Mary and Joseph sit on the bench by the manger. Number 9 contains a carol. Suggested ones include 'Away in a manger'; 'Silent night'.)*

Narration

Mary and Joseph have found a safe place to stay in Bethlehem, and Mary's baby is born. But what's in gift number 10? Oh, there seem to be a number of these. Could you all open them at once, please, and put on the contents (a pair of sunglasses). You don't usually need sunglasses in the middle of the night, do you? On this particular night these shepherds could have done with them. A bright light shocked and scared them! But then they heard that angel again with an amazing message...

Reading Luke 2:8–16

Carol

The shepherds couldn't wait to get to Bethlehem. As they hurry on their way, let's sing. Let's open gift number 11 to find out which carol we will sing. (*Suggested carols include 'See amid the winter's snow'; 'While shepherds watched'. As the congregation sings, the shepherds are encouraged to come forward and gather on the dais. It may be suitable for them to sit on the floor.)*

Narration

On that very special night, the baby was born and had his first visitors. But others came to visit too. Let's open gifts number 12 (a horoscope page, a travel brochure and a map). These wise men (*Indicate the people who opened the gifts.*) want to travel. Here is a travel brochure to prove it. How are they to decide where to go? Is the horoscope page a clue? Some people today use these pages as a guide through life, and the wise men did study the stars, of course. Following horoscopes can confuse us and lead us astray. A map seems a much more sensible guide. Remember, the wise men took a wrong turning and ended up at Herod's palace. It was only when they studied God's word that they got back on track.

Reading Matthew 2:1–11

Carol

Let's sing about the wise men. Please open gift number 13. As we sing could our wise men make their way to Bethlehem. *(Suggested carols include 'We three kings'; 'As with gladness'; 'He is here'. The 'wise men' come forward and stand around the manger.)*

Narration

So here is our story. Here are the small group of people gathered together in Bethlehem watching God's purposes being fulfilled. As we pray, let's think about the people in the story.

Prayer

Prayer leader(s): Let us pray.
Mary and Joseph were people in a country under occupation. The Romans ruled them and told them what to do. They had little or no say about their circumstances. They were moved around at the whim of an Emperor.

We pray for those with no voice, who cannot decide where they live, who are oppressed by forces beyond their control. We ask that we will remember them, and be their voice when we can.

The innkeeper had little to offer, but gave what he could. We thank you, Lord, for those who share what they have, whether it be little or much, with others. Help us to be like them.

The shepherds were poor people who lived ordinary lives, but their lives were changed and their vision was transformed on that night.

We praise you for the way you transform the lives of ordinary people. We pray for Christians all over the world as they live for you, and we ask that you will give them vision as they tell others about you.

The wise men were people who were searching, looking for meaning in life. We pray for all those who are dissatisfied, and are searching for the truth. We pray that they won't be confused by the things of the world, but will find Jesus, the source of all truth.

We ask all these prayers in the name of the Lord Jesus, who came on that first Christmas Day. Amen.

Narration

Well, that is our story. A story of more than 2,000 years ago, but a story for us today too. However, you may have noticed that something is missing. We have two more gifts to open. What might be in them? (Hopefully, someone will suggest the fact that no baby has been put into the tableau.) Let's open gift number 14 (a rubbish sack). Now, there's a surprise! A rubbish sack! But it's something we certainly need, with all this used wrapping paper around. If we were expecting something else in that parcel, we need not be disappointed. The real gift has been here all the time! It is too big to put in a box and has already been given to us. It is Jesus, the Son of God, given at that first Christmas.

To make our picture complete, we will use a doll to represent Jesus in our manger here. *(Produce the doll, or alter the script to ask for a real baby!)*

But what will we do with the real Jesus? Will we clear him away with all these boxes at the end of the service? Will he be put out with the rubbish, when Christmas is over? Joseph and Mary, the shepherds and the wise men, all recognised who he was. What about us?

Prayer

Mary and Joseph, the shepherds and the wise men were people who listened to God, and made Jesus the focus of their attention at that first Christmas. Dear Lord, we pray that this Christmas we might be like them, putting you in the centre of our celebrations, in the centre of our lives. Amen.

Carol

As we think about who Jesus is, why he came and what he means to each one of us, let's sing our last carol from box number 15. As we sing, any children not yet involved might like to come and sit around the manger. *(Suggested carols include 'What kind of greatness'; 'What child is this?'; 'See him lying on a bed of straw'.)*

Blessing

And so may we wish you a very happy Christmas, with Jesus, the best gift of all, in the centre of it. May God the Father bless and keep you, may Jesus the Son shine his light upon you, and may God the Holy Spirit give you wisdom and peace this Christmas time and for ever. Amen.

See, he's here!

A Christmas Day service by Christine Wright

Preparation

You will need: *four foil, gas-filled balloons attached to ribbons or strings long enough to stretch from floor to ceiling. Attach weights and tie one of the following labels to the bottom of each ribbon: 'What shall I do?';. 'Who can help me?'; 'I'm frightened';. 'Fighting and arguments'. Now tie another label to each string at the top (in the same order): 'Wonderful Advisor'; 'Mighty God'; 'Everlasting Father'; 'Prince of Peace' (or the titles in your Bible version of Isaiah 9:6). Pack the balloons in four separate boxes and gift-wrap. Make stars from card (one per household) and hang them from a Christmas tree (or pack into another box).*

Music

Opening hymn

'Joy to the world'; 'Mighty God'

Worship songs

'Come and join the celebration'; 'For unto us a child is born'; 'I worship you, Almighty God'; 'See him lying on a bed of straw'

Closing hymn

'And he shall reign forever'; 'Hark, the herald angels sing'; 'O come all you faithful'

Welcome

Greet everyone with a 'Happy Christmas'. What does that really mean? What kind of happiness are we wishing for, eg good company, peace? Sing a carol that encourages everyone to worship this Christmas Day, eg 'Good Christians all, rejoice'.

Opening prayer

Thank God for all the good things that happen at Christmas. Ask for God's help and forgiveness if we are struggling. Ask for the presence of Jesus in today's worship and celebrations.

Presents received

Ask those who have already opened some Christmas presents to say what they have received. Show the four 'presents' which the church has received: they are something to help us think about the meaning of Christmas, and we will open them later in the service.

Bible reading

Isaiah 9:2–5. Introduce the reading: God promised his people a new start. Good things would start to happen and the bad things would end.

All-age talk

An end to...

Outline briefly the changes that God promised to make, through the prophet Isaiah, stressing the bad things that would end (sadness, oppression, wars, fighting). What are the good things we wish one another, and for the world at Christmas? What are the bad things we would like to put an end to this Christmas? (Encourage people to list not only the 'world' concerns such as war and conflict, but also personal and domestic concerns.) Write them on a large piece of paper at the front. Alternatively, distribute slips of paper and pens, and invite people in small groups to write them down. While music plays or a suitable hymn is sung ('O little town of Bethlehem' or 'Tell out, my soul'), the paper or slips of paper can be put into a plastic bin liner and ceremoniously dumped outside the building.

A new start...

The 'bright light' (Isaiah 9:2) God promised was fulfilled in the coming of Jesus. It would bring great joy to everyone – this was the message of the angels to those shepherds in Bethlehem. Read Luke 2:6–20 or gather the smallest children and tell this part of the Christmas story very simply, using pictures if possible. Sing a simple carol based on this passage, eg 'Away in a manger' or 'While shepherds watched their flocks'.

God's gift...

Now invite some of the children to open the boxes and release the balloons. Find adult volunteers to read out the words at the bottom of the strings. These are like our lists of things we'd like to end at Christmas! God wants to get rid of them, too! His solution was to send his own Son, Jesus, to earth, to live with us. (Many Christmas carols have lines about coming down to earth from above. Using their carol sheets, people could find references to this.) It's important to remember at Christmas that God sent Jesus to us: we don't have to earn his presence, or win a right to go to heaven. Instead God came down to us on earth. Sing a carol about Jesus coming to earth, eg 'Love came down at Christmas' or 'See, amid the winter's snow'.

A new beginning...

When Jesus came to earth, God gave human beings a new start. He dealt with wrong things (give examples) that we couldn't deal with ourselves. And he promised this long before Jesus was born. Read Isaiah 9:6,7. The baby born to be our leader and to right our wrongs came to deal with the things we read on the labels of our balloons (try to give concrete examples which relate to young and old for each label). Now ask four volunteers to pull down the balloons one by one and read the labels at the top: 'Wonderful Advisor'; 'Mighty God'; 'Everlasting Father'; 'Prince of Peace'.

Prayer

Loving God, thank you for sending your Son Jesus to help us.
We need a Wonderful Advisor to be with us, Thank you for Jesus.
We need a Mighty God to be with us, Thank you for Jesus.
We need an Everlasting Father to be with us, Thank you for Jesus.
We need the Prince of Peace to be with us, Thank you for Jesus.
We give you our thanks today and for ever. Amen.

Taking the light home

Now point out the stars on the tree (or in the fifth box): God's promise was that Jesus would be a bright light in a dark world. Invite each household to take a star home, and to think about which of the four titles given to Jesus they need most at the moment. Suggest they place theirs somewhere special to help them remember Christ's presence in their home throughout the Christmas period.

Christmas blessing

Almighty God,
As the people who walked in darkness saw a great light, may we live in your light. As that light gave them joy and hope, give us the joy and hope that comes from knowing you. And as we take your light, joy, and hope into our homes, our church and community this Christmas, help us become more like the Son we worship. Amen.

Immanuel

Immanuel
God with us,
Came to live upon this earth,
To show us that he loved us,
And what human life is worth;
That the homeless have a value,
That he knows the refugee.
Immanuel,
God with us,
Came to live with you and me.

Immanuel
God with us,
Used the touch of human hand,

Reaching outcast, blessing children,
Helping blind and lame to stand;
And his love was shown still further
As they nailed him to a tree.
Immanuel,
God with us,
Came to die for you and me.

Immanuel
God with us,
Is still close by today,
For by his Holy Spirit he has never gone away.
But one day there'll be glory
That every eye shall see;
Immanuel,
God with us,
Will return for you and me.

Poem © Marjory Francis 2000

79

The greatest gift!

An all-age service for the Sunday after Christmas by Helen Franklin

Beforehand, draw a simple row of four presents, and one separate, single gift on to red card and cut up into a strip. Draw a label on each gift, and write on 'This Christmas', 'This year', 'Next year' and 'From me'. Copy enough strips for everyone to have a row of these gifts plus a separate 'From me' gift.

Welcome everyone, especially any visitors.

Carol 'O come, all you faithful'

What was the most popular present this Christmas? (Discover from amongst the congregation.) What was the best present this Christmas? (Ask a few people.)

Your best present may not have been an actual gift but something that happened – or rather, didn't! One family I know celebrated their first Christmas for four years without anyone being ill and said that that was a wonderful gift!

But what has been God's greatest gift to you this Christmas?

The strip of card with 'presents' on it that you were given as you entered church is to help you to think about what God has given to you.

At Christmas we celebrate God's gift of Jesus; his coming to earth to show us how much God loves us; his life of love and care, teaching people about his heavenly Father, and making them better when they were ill; his death on the cross so that all our wrong might be forgiven, and his rising to life again so that we know for sure that it's all dealt with, and that we can be 'best friends' with God for ever.

But year by year as we celebrate the birth of Jesus, some part of it may strike us in a new way, or seem especially important to us.

You may have been challenged by Joseph's willing obedience to take Mary as his wife after the dream where God reassured him; or by the shepherd's response of worship on seeing the newborn son of God. It might be Mary's deep thinking after their visit that has struck you, or the willingness of the wise men to explore and to leave behind the familiar in order to find Jesus.

Perhaps it's Jesus himself who makes the deepest impact on you, who comes as light in darkness, as Immanuel, God with us, as Prince of Peace to a troubled world. It's not just the 'men of strife' who need to 'hush their noise', as one carol says, but all of us who need to stop, now the rush of things is over, and take time and space to think about Christmas.

What has been God's greatest gift to you this Christmas? You may want to write it on the 'gift' as a reminder. Whatever it is, take time to thank him for it, and enjoy it.

Prayer of thanksgiving

You could use some ideas from the congregation to form a prayer of thanks.

Carol 'Come and join the celebration'

Reading Matthew 2:1–12

This time of year is the season of review programmes, as everyone looks back over the best bits of 'their' year and reminds us of the most important events on the news, the funniest things that have happened or the best bits of their programme. We will all have our own particular memories of the year, but sadly they won't always be the ones that we would describe as highlights. Often other things crowd in, things that we might rather forget, and swamp our memories of what has been good.

In the reading from Matthew's gospel, did you notice that just three of the verses covered the remarkable moment when the travellers brought out their unusual gifts for Jesus? The rest of the verses are about King Herod.

Like the wise men, you may have had to make a 'careful search' through the last year to find God's gift to you; circumstances may have made it a difficult year rather than a good one.

You may have read the piece of writing entitled 'Footprints', where someone dreams of walking across sand with God, looking at footprints, and is aware that at the hardest time there is only one set of prints. Asking why God has left them alone then, they receive the answer: 'That was where I carried you'.

That may have been your experience in hard times. If so, thank God for the knowledge of his presence. But it may be that you have had difficult times and yet felt alone, uncarried, struggling. Search carefully through the year to see what God has done for you. In what ways have you seen him at work? What signs have you seen of his love for you? Search amidst the disappointments, fears, dramas and worries, because he has been there and he does love you. Look for God's gift to you and hold fast to it. The Bible promises God's unfailing love; cling on to it, and to him.

Carol 'As with gladness, men of old'

The new year starts in a few days from now. I wonder what it holds for you? I can think back to some years where I'm glad I didn't know what was in store for me in the weeks to come. It doesn't always do to know what's ahead! But a new year is a gift from God; like a new writing book at school, that I always wanted to keep clean and tidy and neat, I begin the new year with hopes that I will do things well.

But what do you want God to give to you this year? It's not wrong to know and to ask. Jesus said to the blind man, Bartimaeus, 'What do you want me to do for you?' Parents here, did you mind being asked for things – or told what your children wanted for Christmas? And children, weren't you excited that you could ask them – and even more thrilled when you received what you wanted? God is our heavenly father who is happy to be asked for things. Let's get one thing clear, he's not a heavenly Father Christmas to whom we present a wish list and then try to be good boys and girls.

But what do you want from God? Does it please God that you want it? Is it a desire that he has placed in you? Or is it a promise that he has given to you? If he has promised it then he will give it, in his own good and right time.

Simeon knew that he would one day see the Lord's Messiah; the Holy Spirit had promised that to him. And when Mary and Joseph brought Jesus to the temple, the promise was more than fulfilled as Simeon held the baby in his arms. What has God promised to you? Keep your eyes open to look for it.

Anna had had no such promise, but spent her days at the temple worshipping God. She was in the right place to be given an unexpected gift from God when she too saw the baby Jesus.

What do you want God to do this year? Keep your eyes and ears open for his gift to you. The apostle Paul, writing to the Ephesians, said that God is 'able to do immeasurably more than all that we can ask or imagine.' So let's ask.

We have deliberately looked more at what God has and will give us; sometimes we get the balance wrong by not recognising his love and kindness to us, but focus all our attention on what we can do for him. But it is right to look at that too; so in response to what God has given to you, what do you want to give to him?

The answer will be unique for each of us. In a moment we will sing 'If I were a shepherd, I would bring a lamb'. That might remind us to bring to God our everyday living; it doesn't have to be a spectacular gift, but can be an everyday thing – what we want to and can give.

'If I were a wise man I would do my part'. Do it – don't hold back, worrying that who you are and what you can give is not good enough.

'What can I give? Give my heart.' Love, serve, obey, honour, follow, show God to others. In a moment of quiet, talk it over with God.

Prayers

God our Father, what gift do we want you to bring to the world this year?
We want peace: the end of wars; for people to live in harmony, to care for one another regardless of racial origin or religious or political beliefs, or of differing views and opinions. Jesus, Prince of Peace, come among us in your power and love. Warm cold hearts to be willing to live together and to accept one another. Sharpen dull minds to find peaceful solutions to problems. Enliven hands that hold weapons to reach out, even to enemies, in love and compassion. And teach us all to treat others as brothers.
What gift do we want you to give to those whose lives are dark and hopeless?
We want you to bring light, hope, people to walk with them in trouble, to hold their hands and to remind them of your love for them; to weep with them when they mourn but to sing with them too when they rejoice.
Jesus, Light of the World, shine your light into these lives. Give strength to face troubles, courage to tackle what is dreaded and the comfort of your presence at all times.
What gift do we want you to give to those whom we love? And to ourselves?
Stir our minds to think of these things and our hearts to work for them.
Jesus, friend of sinners, baby of Bethlehem, Son of God, you asked a blind man, 'What do you want me to do for you?' We have told you. Please give us the patience and faith of Simeon to wait for these things, and to trust you in the coming year. As an act of trust we say together the Lord's Prayer.

Carol 'If I were a shepherd'

You may not know yet what your gift to God should be; keep on thinking about it. As the offering boxes are passed round, you may want to put in a gift of money, but as a sign of your love for him, would you put in the separate 'from me' card to symbolise your gift to God.

Carol 'Hark! The Herald' The offering can be taken during this carol.

Blessing

81

Creative prayers for Christmas

Christmas prayer ideas by Judith Merrell

Christmas gift of praise

'Now, our God, we give you thanks, and praise your glorious name.' 1 Chronicles 29:13

You will need: *a large, empty gift-wrapped box; ribbon, sticky labels or slips of paper and glue sticks*

At Christmas we all exchange presents with one another, so why not make a gift of praise for Jesus? Wrap a cardboard box in Christmas paper and tie a bright ribbon around it. (Alternatively paste a large square of gift wrap onto backing paper and add ribbons to make a 2D present.) Next, give out small pieces of paper or sticky labels and ask the group to each draw or write something that they want to thank or praise Jesus for this Christmas time. Play some quiet music while people come up one at a time to stick their prayers on to the gift box. Finish by lifting the box high and offering this gift of praise to Jesus in a concluding prayer.

Prayer paper chain

'Be joyful always, pray at all times, be thankful in all circumstances' 1 Thessalonians 5:16–18

You will need: *strips of coloured paper, pens and felt-tip pens, staplers*

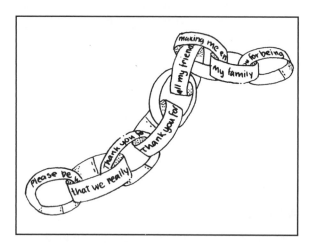

Give each member of the group a strip of coloured paper and encourage them to write a one-line thank you prayer thanking God for the gift of his son, Jesus, on that first Christmas. Fasten all the strips together with a stapler to make a festive paper chain that you can hang across your meeting room. If you only have a small group, you might want to give each person two or three strips of paper or add to

the chain week by week. It is great fun to make a prayer paper chain during an all-age service when a long chain can be made and hung right across the church.

Holly wreath

'She gave birth to her first son, wrapped him in strips of cloth and laid him in a manger – there was no room for them to stay in the inn.' Luke 2:7

You will need: *green paper holly leaves; large ring of card; small red circles; pens; glue*

Many people hang a welcoming wreath on their door at Christmas time. Why not make a similar wreath to hang on the door of your church or meeting room? When Jesus was born he didn't receive a warm welcome inside the inn – his expectant mother was sent round to the stable at the back. Make a point of welcoming Jesus to your Christmas celebrations this year.

Give out the paper holly leaves and ask the group to write short prayers on them, inviting Jesus to be a part of their Christmas celebrations, or thanking God for his special gift. Suggest that young children draw a picture of themselves with their arms open in welcome. Stick all the prayers on to the circle of card and add a few red paper berries. Attach a ribbon and hang the prayer collage on your door. Finish by reading out some of the prayers and dedicating the wreath to God.

Christmas stars

'Let us thank God for his priceless gift.'
2 Corinthians 9:15

You will need: *scissors, card, star template, glitter, glue, pens, hole punch, thin ribbon*

Use the star shape illustrated to make several cardboard templates. Have ready some sheets of thin card so that each member of the group can draw round a template and cut out their own star. Then, invite your group to write one-line thank you prayers thanking God for Christmas and for the gift of his son. Decorate the edges of the prayer stars with glitter, then punch a hole in the top of each one and attach a piece of ribbon, so that they can be hung on a Christmas tree. If your church has its own tree, why not encourage group members to make two decorations: one to take home and one for the church tree.

For more creative prayer ideas check out *One Hundred and One Ideas for Creative Prayer,* ISBN 0 86201 954 0 or *New Ideas for Creative Prayer,* ISBN 1 85999 589 6 both by Judith Merrell and both published by Scripture Union.

It's Jesus' birthday!

'This very day in David's town your Saviour was born – Christ the Lord!'
Luke 2:11

You will need: *an OHP, blank acetate and pen or a large sheet of paper and marker pen*

Ask the group to help you make a long list of all the things that need to be done before Christmas. Draw out that all of these jobs can make us forget the true meaning of Christmas. Sometimes we are so busy getting ready for Christmas that we forget all about Jesus whose birthday we are celebrating. Weave all of the jobs on your list into a simple response prayer and invite the group to join in with the response. The prayer might sound something like this...

As we go shopping and choose gifts...

Lord Jesus, help us to remember that we're celebrating your birthday.

As we write cards and wrap presents...

As we bake cakes and make mince pies...

As we put up our tree and decorate our home...

Christmas stocking

'Then the ones who pleased the Lord will ask, "When did we give you something to eat or drink? When did we welcome you as a stranger or give you clothes to wear or visit you while you were sick or in jail?" The King will answer, "Whenever you did it for any of my people, no matter how unimportant they seemed, you did it for me."' Matthew 25:37–40 CEV

You will need: *a Christmas stocking, pens and slips of paper*

At Christmas it is easy to exchange cards and gifts with each other and forget the person whose birthday it really is. Can you imagine how you'd feel if it was your birthday, and everyone else received a present but you? Explain that this stocking is going to be a special gift for Jesus. Of course we can't give Jesus anything face to face, but Jesus said that anything we do for someone in need we do for him (see verse above).

Ask the group to think about whether they could give a little of their time, money, talents or prayers to help someone else. They should then write their idea on their slip of paper and pop it into the Christmas stocking as a gift for Jesus. For example: I'll take some mince pies to my elderly neighbour. I'll offer to give Mrs Johnson a lift to church. I''ll give the toys that I've outgrown to a charity shop. I'll pack up a box for the shoe-box appeal. I'll look after Jane's children while she goes shopping.

Conclude with a short prayer offering the whole stocking and all that it contains to Jesus.

Christmas theme games

Christmas trees

One or two children are 'on' (or more if it's a big room!) and when they tag someone, that person becomes a Christmas tree: they must stand still with their arms out until someone who is still running free runs right round them once to free them. Play several times so lots of children are 'on'.

Sleeping children

A good game when you want to calm things down. As in the game 'Sleeping lions' everyone lies down on the floor, as if it's Christmas Eve and they are trying to go to sleep. An adult goes round checking to see that nobody moves! (If little ones really fall asleep, leave them for a while!)

Christmas is coming

As in the game 'Port starboard' or 'Captain's on the deck', call out words that require specific actions, eg hang the decorations (reach up high, standing on tiptoe, as if hanging baubles on a tree); Father Christmas! (lie still as if asleep); reindeer (make hands into 'antlers' on heads and trot round); jingle bells (dance round in a circle); Christmas tree (stand still with arms out at sides); snowmen (stand totally still in any position).

Nazareth to Bethlehem

Similar to 'Christmas is coming' but using biblical details, eg one wall is Nazareth, the opposite is Bethlehem; the wall to the right of Bethlehem is Herod's palace and the wall to the left is the stable. Instructions could include: clean the stable (scrub the floor); camels (crawl on hands and knees with a humped back); rock the baby (stand still and rock a baby); manger (lie on back with legs and arms in the air); follow the star (walk round pointing upwards) etc.

Christmas corners

Label the four corners of the room with Christmas words, eg 'Snowmen', 'Reindeer', 'Presents' and 'Cards'. Prepare four small cards, one with each word on it, and fold them in half. Encourage everyone to dance round the room to some suitable seasonal music. When the music stops the children choose a corner and run to it. Someone then chooses one of the cards and reads out the word on it. Whoever is standing in that corner is 'out' for one go.

What's the time, Santa Claus?

This game is a variation on 'What's the time, Mr Wolf?' All the children line up at one end of the room while another child or leader stands at the opposite end of the room with their back to the others, playing the part of Santa. The group calls out, 'What's the time, Santa Claus?' and Santa replies, 'Two o'clock' or 'Five o'clock' or any time that comes into their head. The whole group takes the appropriate number of steps according to the time that is called out. When Santa shouts out 'Midnight, and you should be asleep!', all the children race back to their wall pursued by Santa. Whoever Santa manages to catch becomes the next Santa in his place.

Pin the nose on Rudolph

Play a variation of the game 'Pin the tail on the donkey'. Have a large picture of Rudolph the reindeer without his red nose. Have a separate, large cardboard nose with a blob of Blu-tack on the back. Blindfold the children, one at a time, and turn them round three times, before standing them in front of the picture and letting them attempt to fix the nose to the right place. Award a small prize to the child that comes the nearest. Try 'Pin the star to the top of the Christmas tree' as an alternative.

Some of these games could be played as elimination games, where the last to do an action etc is 'out'. Children can get bored in these situations so why not use the 'out for one go' method? This prevents bored children getting naughty too!

Five simple recipes – the first four don't even require an oven!

Mini chocolate logs

You will need: *mini chocolate Swiss rolls; chocolate icing; icing sugar; sieve; paper plates; birthday candles and holder; teaspoons; blunt knives; forks; small decorations*

Give children a chocolate mini roll on a paper plate and help them to cover it with chocolate icing. Gently drag a fork through the icing to give the effect of tree bark, then sieve a little icing sugar over the top to look like snow. Add one or two small decorations and a birthday candle in a holder. Light the candles and thank God that he sent Jesus to be the light of the world, then enjoy a refreshment break together.

 Always take care when using candles with children. Have a bowl of water ready to put all the candles into.

Epiphany biscuits

You will need: *plain biscuits or small cakes; a dish of white icing; small sweets, eg chocolate buttons or jellies; paper plates; teaspoons; blunt knives*

Mix up some white icing. While you are doing this, tell the group about the Christmas tradition of celebrating Epiphany (the arrival of the wise men) with cakes decorated with a crown.

Give each child a cake or biscuit on a paper plate and help them to spread icing over the top of it and then decorate it with a circle of sweets to make a crown.

Christmas pudding truffles

You will need: *50 g butter or margarine pre-creamed together with 125 g icing sugar; 30 g cocoa; 2 ml vanilla essence; 30 ml double cream; 250 g crushed trifle sponges; aprons; wooden spoons; large bowl; small cake cases; plates*
To decorate: *chocolate sugar strands; icing sugar; tiny sprigs of artificial holly*

Let the children take it in turns to add or stir in the ingredients in the order listed. Divide the mixture between the children and help them to roll it into walnut-size balls. Sprinkle chocolate strands on a plate and let the children roll their ball of mixture in the strands until well coated. Sieve icing sugar over the top of each pudding to look like snow and decorate with a sprig of artificial holly. This mixture makes 16 truffles.

For Australian Christmas Pudding, stir together a large container of vanilla ice cream with 5 g of cinnamon and 15 g each of two or three dried fruits (or small sweets). Consume immediately!

Crispy chocolate mangers

You will need: *a saucepan; boiling water; a thick cloth, eg a towel; a Pyrex dish (the right size to sit in the top of the saucepan); wooden spoon; 110 g cooking chocolate; three crumbled Shredded Wheats; paper cake cases; jelly babies; ready-to-roll white icing; icing sugar; plates*

Away from the children, pour boiling water into the saucepan and wrap it well in the thick cloth to preserve the heat and to prevent the children from burning themselves. Fix a Pyrex dish into the top of the saucepan so that it sits just above the water. Ask the children to break the chocolate into small pieces and drop them into the dish. Stir the chocolate as it melts. Crumble the Shredded Wheats and add a spoonful at a time, mixing well to coat with chocolate.

Spoon into paper cake cases, but instead of heaping the mixture up, make a dent for the 'baby' to be added later. Leave to cool and set.

Pinch off small pieces of fondant icing for the children to roll out. Sprinkle icing sugar on the work surface to prevent sticking. Wrap this 'blanket' around a jelly baby and then place the baby into the chocolate crispy manger.

Gingerbread stars

You will need: *115 g sugar; 420 g plain flour; 1 tsp of bicarbonate of soda; 2 tsp of ground ginger; 125 g butter; 4 tsp golden syrup; 1 egg lightly whisked; currants and glacé cherries for decoration; aprons; bowl; star cookie cutters; wooden spoons; scales; sieve; 2 baking trays*

Sift the flour, bicarbonate of soda and ginger into a bowl. Rub in the butter. Add the sugar and mix well. Warm the syrup and add with the egg to the other ingredients. Knead till smooth. Roll out on a floured surface to a thickness of 3 mm and then cut into star shapes with the cutters. Lift the biscuits on to a lightly greased tray. Decorate the star biscuits with currants and/or glacé cherries. Bake in a moderate oven for 8–10 minutes or until golden brown.

 Be aware of food allergies. Check that all the children are safe to handle and eat the ingredients.

Christmas quiz

Choose about 20 of the following questions to suit the age and style of your group. The key to a good quiz is to keep it short and sweet! Questions marked with a ✪ are intended for younger children

Tip! Why not use a random method of scoring? Have about 20 cut-out star shapes with a score of 5, 10 or 20 marked on the back. Fix all the stars to your score sheet with Blu-tack. Each time a team answers a question correctly they can choose a star, and turn it over to reveal their score.

1 'With logs on the fire and gifts on the tree' is a line from which Christmas single? *'Mistletoe and Wine' by Cliff Richard*
2 What does 'Advent' mean? *'Coming'*
3 How many sides does a snowflake have? *6 or 8, including front and back, it depends on how devious you're feeling!*
4 How soon after Mary and Joseph reached Bethlehem was Jesus born? *We don't know!*
5 Which coin was traditionally put in a Christmas pudding? *A sixpence*
6 From which town did Mary and Joseph travel to Bethlehem? *Nazareth*
7 ✪ What would you normally find at the top of a Christmas tree? *Angel or star*
8 When was the first Christmas card sent? *1843*
9 Name two people whom angels spoke to in the Christmas story. *Mary, Joseph, shepherds*
10 Who was king when Jesus was born? *Herod*
11 The Trafalgar Square Christmas tree is a gift to London from which city? *Oslo, Norway*
12 Joseph was descended from which king's line? *David*
13 ✪ What would you find inside a Christmas cracker? *Hat, joke, gift, 'snap'*
14 How many wise men were there? *We don't know, although many people assume there were three because three different gifts are mentioned*
15 How soon after Jesus' birth did the wise men arrive? *We don't know, but it was probably some months later*
16 Can you name a UK Christmas number one with the word 'Christmas' in the title? *'Merry Xmas Everybody' – Slade (spelling allowed!); 'Lonely This Christmas' – Mud; 'Do They Know It's Christmas?' – Band Aid/Band Aid II; 'Merry Christmas Everyone' – Shakin' Stevens*
17 Where did Mary and Joseph take the baby Jesus to when they escaped from Herod? *Egypt*
18 What is hidden inside the traditional Christmas dessert rice porridge in Scandinavia? *An almond*
19 What is said to happen for the girl who finds it? *She will be the next bride*

20 What gifts did the wise men bring to Jesus? *Gold, frankincense and myrrh*
21 How many reindeer pull Father Christmas' sleigh? *Eight*
22 Which prophet said 'A virgin will have a baby boy, and he will be called Immanuel'? *Isaiah*
23 What does 'Immanuel' mean? *'God with us'*
24 Which group had the UK Christmas number one with the same single in two separate years, and what was the song? *Queen, 'Bohemian Rhapsody'*
25 Which country does the striped candy cane come from? *USA*
26 How did the wise men find the baby Jesus? *They followed a star*
27 What strange ingredient would you have found in plum porridge, an early version of Christmas pudding? *Beef*
28 How did the wise men know they had to go home another way? *They were warned in a dream*
29 Which play has been produced in London every Christmas since 1904? *Peter Pan*
30 Which group had the UK Christmas number one for three consecutive years? *The Spice Girls, 1996, 1997, 1998*
31 (link to **30**) Can you name the songs? *'2 Become 1', 'Too Much', 'Goodbye'*
32 Which Bible characters would you find in a traditional Christmas crib/nativity scene? *Jesus, Mary, Joseph, the ox, the ass, shepherds, sheep, the three wise men*
33 ✪ Where did Mary put the newborn baby Jesus? *In a manger*
34 What does the word 'nativity' mean? *Birth*
35 ✪ What does Father Christmas say? *'Ho, ho, ho!'*
36 What's another name for Father Christmas? *Santa Claus, Saint Nicholas*
37 ✪ What might you go and see at the theatre over Christmas? *A pantomime*
38 ✪ Which of Father Christmas' reindeer has a red nose? *Rudolph*
39 'The cattle are lowing, the baby awakes' is a line from which carol? *'Away in a manger'*
40 Name three things you might hang on your Christmas tree. *Baubles, tinsel, angel, star, lights, chocolate decorations, ornaments...*
41 Where might two people enjoy a Christmas kiss? *Under the mistletoe*
42 Who always gives a speech on Christmas Day? *The Queen*
43 Name two things you might eat at Christmas. *Turkey, cranberry sauce, sprouts!, Christmas pudding, mince pies, Christmas cake, Yule log...*
44 When would you open the first door of your Advent calendar? *1 December*
45 What is the day after Christmas Day called? *Boxing Day*
46 'Sleep in heavenly peace' is a line from which Christmas carol? *'Silent night'*

Spot the difference

Find the ten differences in this Christmas spot the difference!

Christmas tree wordsearch

Read the Christmas story below and then find the bold words in our Christmas tree wordsearch

Mary and **Joseph** travelled all the way from their home in **Nazareth** to **Bethlehem** to be registered for the King's head count. Mary was expecting a very important **baby**. An **angel** had told her that this baby would be the **Son** of **God**.

Mary and Joseph couldn't find a **room** anywhere in Bethlehem, but an innkeeper let them stay in the stable at the back of his **inn** and this is where Mary gave birth to baby **Jesus**.

That **night**, in the fields near Bethlehem, some **shepherds** were watching their **sheep**. Suddenly an angel appeared to them and told them about the **birth** of this special baby. The shepherds rushed into town to see Jesus. They found him in a stable, lying in a **manger**, just as the angel had told them.

Later some **wise men** followed a new **star** and travelled a long way to come and worship Jesus.

At Christmas we celebrate Jesus' birthday.

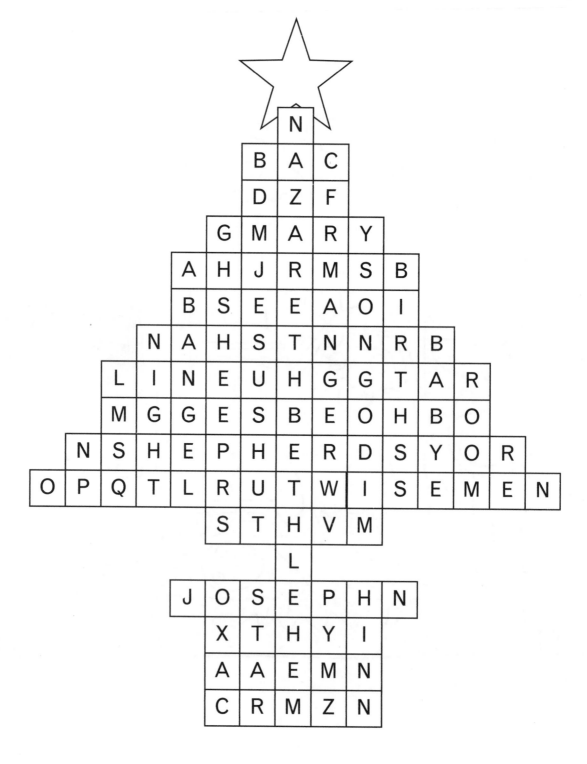

BELLS
FAMILY
TINSEL
PRESENTS
DECORATIONS
TREE
TELEVISION
CHOCOLATE
STOCKING
REINDEER

CAROLS
TURKEY
PUDDING·
CRACKERS
CANDLE
HOLY SPIRIT
IMMANUEL
MESSIAH
MARY
JOSEPH

WISE MEN
BETHLEHEM
BABY
JESUS
KING OF THE JEWS
ANGEL
SON
GOLD
FRANKINCENSE
MYRRH

W	E	S	T	D	S	C	R	A	C	K	E	R	S	T	X
F	A	M	I	L	Y	T	I	N	A	Y	F	A	W	R	L
R	E	I	N	O	P	Z	A	R	N	E	L	L	I	E	B
A	C	H	O	G	O	L	N	E	D	K	B	F	S	Q	I
N	P	U	D	D	I	N	G	I	L	R	N	N	E	M	S
K	L	K	J	F	T	N	E	N	E	U	I	U	M	U	W
I	A	L	H	I	I	I	L	D	B	T	T	A	E	J	E
N	E	O	T	K	K	T	R	E	M	W	N	F	N	A	J
C	H	O	C	O	L	A	T	E	V	U	C	A	R	O	E
E	J	O	A	B	T	R	E	R	E	S	O	J	P	U	H
N	T	L	R	E	C	H	O	L	Y	S	P	I	R	I	T
S	B	M	O	T	B	M	N	G	Y	O	K	E	E	U	F
E	J	C	L	H	X	E	Q	Z	C	N	R	R	S	M	O
E	E	O	S	L	Y	S	L	A	M	A	T	T	E	R	G
L	S	O	S	H	L	S	D	L	M	A	R	Y	N	O	N
E	U	L	R	E	L	I	N	E	S	B	E	B	T	C	I
T	S	R	A	I	P	A	G	E	R	Y	L	A	S	U	K
H	Y	R	N	M	E	H	E	L	H	T	E	B	S	W	Y
M	I	D	E	C	O	R	A	T	I	O	N	S	T	H	A
W	J	E	L	L	T	E	L	E	V	I	S	I	O	N	X

Christmas quotes and anecdotes

Why not use some of these illustrations to enliven your talks, sermons or church magazines?

Three six-year-olds were playing the wise men in the school nativity play. As they came to Mary and Joseph in the stable, the first one handed over his gift and said, 'Gold'. The second one presented his gift and said, 'Myrhh'. The third one threw his gift into the manger and said, 'Frankie sent this.'

Having taught her children about the birth of Jesus, the Sunday school teacher was admiring their efforts to draw the scene. Among the animals, the crib, the shepherds, Mary and Joseph, one little boy had added a small fat man standing close to baby Jesus. Rather reproachfully, the teacher asked if the little boy had added Santa Claus. 'Oh no!' he replied. 'That's Round John Virgin!'

Jesus was laid in a borrowed manger. He preached from a borrowed boat. He fed 5,000 with a borrowed packed lunch. He rode into Jerusalem on a borrowed donkey. He celebrated the Last Supper in a borrowed room. They laid his dead body in a borrowed tomb. Today he still seeks and saves, he preaches and feeds, he blesses and heals – through lives he can borrow.

A child's prayer: Dear God I bet it's very hard for you to love all the people in the world. There are only four people in our family and I can never do it. (David Pytches, *Out of the Mouth of Babes*, Eagle Publishing)

An elephant was splashing about in the river. On the sandy shore, a mouse, watching him, became more and more disturbed. 'Come out of the water at once!' cried the mouse. 'Why?' replied the elephant. The mouse kept on shouting, and in the end, for the sake of peace and quiet, the elephant came out of the water and stood over the mouse. 'Now, why did you want me to come out of the water?' the elephant asked. 'I just wanted to see if you were wearing my swimming costume,' the mouse replied.

It's easier for us to understand how an elephant could wear a mouse's swimming costume than it is for us to understand the mystery of the Incarnation – God's word became flesh. He wore our suit of clothes.

At art college you are taught: 'Never rub out.' Instead you are taught to use what you have and work from it, no matter how unsatisfactory it may be as a starting point. This has been God's approach to his creation. Christmas is a celebration of his determination never to give up on his people, no matter what it takes.

The next best thing to being sure that 'we have found him' is to find another person to whom we can say 'come and see'. **Francis Ridley Havergal**

If you take Christ out of Christmas, all that is left is M & S!

The confusions of the season reached their zenith last week, in my view, when a chorus of adoring school children on television were asked by the teacher, 'Now, who is the most important person at Christmas?' When they carolled, 'Father Christmas!' she said approvingly, 'That's right.' So much for baby Jesus and all that stuff. **Katherine Whitehorn, The** *Observer*

A boy threw a stone at the stained glass window of the nativity. It nicked out the 'e' in the word 'highest' which was part of the text GLORY TO GOD IN THE HIGHEST. Thus, until unfortunately it was mended, it read GLORY TO GOD IN THE HIGH ST. George MacLeod

Try as I might I could not convince him that playing Joseph was a great honour. 'Lots of little boys would love to be Joseph,' I encouraged.

'I want to be a soldier and carry a sword.'

'I don't think there are any soldiers in a nativity play, are there?'

'There are in this one. And they get to wear silver armour. I have to have a stupid tea towel tied round my head with string. I'll look really stupid. And I have to put my arm around

Christmas quotes and anecdotes

90

Jessica Brown and the other boys will say I love her and I DON'T!'

Keeping an arm's length between him and Jessica, he did it, tea towel and all. 'Doing things you don't really want to do is what makes a man of you,' I told him. 'I'm proud of you. We could hear every word and you didn't forget a line.' He grunted. The ordeal was over, thank the Lord. But I wondered whether the real Joseph had been as reluctant to play his part in the first nativity.

> The fact of Jesus' coming is the final and unanswerable proof that God cares. **William Barclay**

Christmas is too large to be tucked away in the toe of a child's stocking. **Gerald Stanley Lee**

> In the school nativity play in which the children had been encouraged to express the story in their own way, the innkeeper having told Mary and Joseph that there was no room at the inn immediately added, 'But come in for a drink anyway.' **James Simpson**, *Holy Wit*

To be happy is the secret of life. To wake up on Christmas morning and know that you are loved makes you very happy. **Penny Knight Hamilton**, aged 12, in *A Child's view of Christmas*, Richard and Helen Exley

> I'm not sure I like this plan. All those hundreds of years of waiting, choirs of angels singing 'Glory to God', moving stars around the universe, the miracle of the Son of God being conceived by a virgin, all these messages we've been taking down about the coming Messiah, all those promises about the people who walked in darkness seeing a great light.

And what have we had so far? The poor parents have had to trudge for days from their home in Nazareth, to finish up having their baby in a second-rate town, in what looks to me very like a stable, fit only for animals, the news is going to be announced to a group of scruffy, ignorant shepherds, hundreds of innocent children are going to be massacred, and our chosen family is going to end up as refugees in, of all

places, Egypt! Aren't there any good bits in the plan? **Derek Haylock**, Celsta's speech from 'Guardian Angels', from *Plays on the Word*.

> He who has no Christmas in his heart will never find Christmas under a tree. **Anon**

Men and women everywhere sigh on 26 December and say they're glad Christmas is over for another year. But it isn't over! 'Unto you is born a Saviour.' It's just beginning and it will go on forever. **Eugenia Price**

> Many people think that it's wrong to call Christmas 'Xmas'. 'It's like taking Christ away from Christmas!' they say. It's a reflection of the way Christmas has become separated from the birthday of Jesus Christ. But let's think about it in another way. When I receive a letter with a row of Xs at the bottom, it tells me that the sender loves me very much. When we see Christmas written 'Xmas' it can remind us that God loves us so much that he sent his own son to tell us. So Xmas starts with a big kiss to remind us of God's great love. And of course an X is also a cross and Jesus' love took him all the way from the stable to the cross. **Judith Merrell**

Songs, rhymes and raps

Christ is born today

A song for all ages to the tune of 'Jingle Bells'

Many years ago,
In a stable far away,
Christ the Lord was born.
What a joyful day!
Singing filled the air,
Glory shone around,
Shepherds on the hillside
Were astonished by this sound.

Have no fear! Have you heard?
Christ is born today.
Go and see him lying there
In a manger filled with hay – hey!
Then the sky came alive,
Angels everywhere
Singing hymns of joyful praise
To the God who sent them there.

On to Bethlehem,
In a most exciting way,
Shepherds went to see
Christ the Lord that day.
When they saw him there
They were filled with joy,
On their knees they worshipped him
God's special baby boy.

Have no fear! Have you heard?
Christ is born today.
Go and see him lying there
In a manger filled with hay – hey!
Then the sky came alive,
Angels everywhere
Singing hymns of joyful praise
To the God who sent them there.

By Peter Graystone and Ray Chering

Wise men rap!

A rap for children aged 7 and older

Set up a rhythm with the children clapping their hands or tapping their knees. Then read the rap one line at a time, and ask the children to repeat the words. Alternatively, divide the group in two and let them rap alternate lines or alternate sections.

Far in the east, they studied the skies.
A new star appeared and dazzled their eyes.
These guys were wise and knew what it meant:
A king had been born; the star marked the event.
They loaded their camels and headed west.
Following the star by night was best.

In Israel they went to Herod the king.
To be born in a palace was just the thing.
But Herod said there was no baby there.
The thought of a new king gave him quite a scare.
He called the leaders and demanded to know
Where the Saviour of Israel would be born, and so,
They told him Bethlehem was the place to look,
For that was written in an ancient book.

Herod told the guys that he would worship too,
So he asked them to find him and send word through.
But God got the word out in the wise guys' dreams
'Don't get caught by that bad guy's evil schemes.'
So they never did come back that way.
They were guided on by the star's bright ray.

They followed the star as it led them on
Until they found Jesus in the house on which it shone.
The wise guys bowed and gave him what they'd brought
The gifts that they'd chosen with lots of thought.
Frankincense, a gift for God, and gold for a king.
Myrhh for a life of pain and suffering.

By Mandy Engelsma

Rap and respond

A rap for children of all ages. Ask a leader or team of older children to chant the verses while the whole group joins in with the words and relevant actions to the chorus

Chorus: Jump up, clap hands, turn round, sit down,
Jump up, clap hands, turn round, sit down.

Now I'm about to tell you 'bout a fabulous star
How it shone like a beacon, led us from afar.
We were just three guys, though we're pretty smart
When we saw that star, it was time to start.

Chorus: Jump up, clap hands, turn round, sit down,
Jump up, clap hands, turn round, sit down.

We had studied all the books, done the homework thing
So we knew we were lookin' for a mighty king.
In the palace in Jerusalem we took a look
Didn't trust that Herod, didn't fit the book.

Chorus: Jump up, clap hands, turn round, sit down,
Jump up, clap hands, turn round, sit down.

It was late at night when the star it stopped
Found Mary and Joseph's place so in we dropped.
Now listen good, 'cause it's the strangest thing
We found a little baby and just wanted to sing.

Chorus: Jump up, clap hands, turn round, sit down,
Jump up, clap hands, turn round, sit down.

From the buzz in our heads and the feeling of joy
We knew it was the king, just a little boy.
So we gave our gifts to the little Lord
Gold, frankincense, myrrh, best we could afford.

Chorus: Jump up, clap hands, turn round, sit down,
Jump up, clap hands, turn round, sit down.

We were warned in a dream to go straight off home
So we took no detour, back the way we'd come.
We felt like singing with our hearts so glad
Told everyone at home about the time we'd had.

Chorus: Jump up, clap hands, turn round, sit down,
Jump up, clap hands, turn round, sit down.

Twinkle, twinkle, star so bright

A song for 3 to 5 year olds to the tune of 'Twinkle, twinkle, little star'

Twinkle, twinkle, star so bright,
Twinkle, twinkle in the night,
Up above the world so high,
Wise men saw you in the sky.
Twinkle, twinkle, star so bright,
Twinkle, twinkle in the night.

Twinkle, twinkle, star so bright,
Twinkle, twinkle in the night,
God sent you to show the way
To the house where Jesus lay.
Twinkle, twinkle, star so bright,
Twinkle, twinkle in the night.

By Margaret Spivey

Be a star

An action rhyme for 3 to 5 year olds

Five bright shining stars twinkling in the sky,
One of them was hidden as a cloud rolled by.

Four bright shining stars twinkling in the sky,
One of them put out its light as the moon rose high.

Three bright shining stars twinkling in the sky,
One of them played hide and seek and vanished from the sky.

Two bright shining stars twinkling in the sky,
One of them has gone to sleep – and so must I.

So that leaves one bright shining star twinkling on and on,
The star the wise men followed till they found God's Son.

By Alison Gidney

Glory!

A song for 2 to 5 year olds to the tune of 'London's burning'

Glory, glory, glory, glory,
Glory, glory, glory, glory,
Peace on earth, peace on earth,
God's Son is born.

By Jean Elliott

So bright!

A song for 3 to 5 year olds to the tune of 'This little light of mine'.

Jesus is the light, shining oh so bright,
Jesus is the light, shining oh so bright,
Jesus is the light, shining oh so bright,
Shining bright, shining bright, he's the light!

By Angela Thompson

Angel rap

An echo chant story for 3 to 7 year olds. A leader chants each line rap style with an accompanying action. The children echo his words and copy the action. Why not fix tinsel around the children's heads and perform the rap for others to enjoy.

We love to sing, (*Hands on heart, then on either side of mouth.*)
Of God's great glory. (*Wiggle fingertips in a large arc.*)
We love to sing, (*Hands on heart, then on either side of mouth.*)
Of God's good news. (*Clap.*)
Don't be afraid, (*Cover then uncover eyes with hands.*)
For God so loves you. (*Hands on heart.*)
Listen to us, (*Cup hand to ear.*)
We've got good news. (*Clap.*)

A baby is born, (Rock arms.)
He's come to help us. *(Shake hands with yourself.)*
A baby is born, *(Rock arms.)*
It's such good news. *(Clap.)*
Glory to God! *(Raise hands while waving.)*
And peace to his people! *(Palms together.)*
Glory to God! *(Raise hands while waving.)*
It's such good news! *(Clap.)*

By Mary Houlgate

Sing good news

A song for 3 to 5 year olds to the tune of 'We wish you a merry Christmas'. Why not sing this verse walking round in a circle holding hands?

An angel came to Mary,
An angel came to Mary,
An angel came to Mary,
To bring her good news.
'Good tidings I bring
Of a new baby king.'
An angel came to Mary
To bring her good news.

By Helen Burn

One night

A song for 3 to 7 year olds to the tune of 'Bobby Shaftoe'

Ask the children to repeat these words, line by line after you:
Joseph had a dream one night,
When an angel, big and bright,
Told him, 'Joseph, it's all right –
You will marry Mary.
She will have a baby son,
He will be God's promised one.
He will love us every one,
And his name is Jesus.'

By Margaret Spivey

Joseph's dream

A song for 3 to 7 year olds to the tune of 'My bonnie lies over the ocean'

When Joseph lay quietly dreaming, *('Sleep' on folded hands.)*
An angel so big and so bright *(Circle arms.)*
Said 'You must be married to Mary, *(Stretch arms out.)*
For that is God's message tonight.
Joseph, Joseph, Mary is having a baby boy; *(Rock arms.)*
Jesus, Jesus, he will be Jesus, her son.'

By Margaret Spivey

Songs, rhymes and raps

For Easter

New material and Scripture Union favourites

Easter cracked

Drama, Craft, Events, Service Outlines,
and everything your church might need for Easter
— well almost everything!

Easter Cracked

£11.99

978 1 84427 189 4

Easter Cracked is a vital resource for churches hoping to make the most of the opportunities they have to reach out during Easter. Contains services, craft, drama and more to use with all-ages.

For other festivals

New material and Scripture Union favourites

Celebrations sorted

Great resources for:
Remembrance Sunday
Mothering Sunday
Pentecost
New Year
Valentine's Day
Harvest
and much, much more!

Celebrations Sorted

£11.99

978 1 84427 182 5

Celebrations Sorted is packed full of ideas for you to use at times of celebration in the church calendar. Includes service outlines, craft, drama, assemblies, creative prayer and much, much more.